SAILING INTO THE ABYSS

SAILING INTO THE ABYSS

A TRUE ADVENTURE STORY

BRIDGET LANE

First Printing, 2012 Goldmineguides.com
© 2012 by BridgetLane
ISBN-10: 1480257001
ISBN-13: 978-1480257009

This book is a work of non-fiction based on the life, experiences and recollections of the author. In some instances, names of people have been changed for artistic purposes and to protect the privacy of others.

Cover Design Judy Marks

DEDICATION

To my sons Albie and Thomas and all the joy they
have brought to my life

ACKNOWLEDGMENTS

I would like to thank my sister Judy and brother Patrick for all their help and support.

I also want to thank the wonderful friends that I have around the world who have made my life so rich and joyful.

CONTENTS

CHAPTER ONE

A LIFE AT SEA

The rain was falling heavily and relentlessly, seeping its way down the neck of my foul-weather gear, soaking my clothes underneath and making me shiver as the water cooled on contact with my skin. Lightning flashed intermittently, illuminating the turbulent sea and white-crested waves that surrounded me. What was I doing here alone on the ocean, steering an ill-equipped boat off a strange coast thousands of miles from my country of birth?

It was November 1980, and I was thirty-one years old; nothing in my youth had pointed toward finding me in this position. I hadn't discovered sailing until I was twenty-four, but having once discovered the joy of sailing and the sense of freedom I felt from the activity, I never wanted to give it up. The summer after my mother died in 1973, my father planned a trip from England to France in his new 24-foot sailboat with my eight-year-old brother and my twelve-year-old sister. For some reason, the logic of which escapes me now, my seventeen-year-old sister Judy and I felt we should accompany them as my father had no sailing experience. Neither had we, but that seemed irrelevant. Amazingly, the voyage took place without serious mishap, despite our learning as we went:

"Look out for something red. Oh no ... hang on, that means rock, not red ... better turn left."

For me, the trip was a revelation as I discovered that, for the first time in twenty-four years, I was relaxed, and I liked it. Sailing then became my life, and I became what is known in the trade as a "yachtie"; that is a person who makes their living working and living on other people's yachts.

Seven years later, I still loved the life but was tired of living out of suitcases. I worked hard both sailing and maintaining boats. I studied and earned my Yachtmaster's Certificate, but finding financial rewards eluded me. On occasional visits to London I would find my old friends, from London and university, pursuing successful professional careers and securing mortgages to buy houses. I didn't envy them, but at times, as I hauled my suitcase filled with all my worldly possessions from boat to boat, I thought how pleasant it would be to have my own boat to go home to between jobs and to house my few possessions in.

The boating world in the 1980s was, and still is, a male-dominated world where women find work mainly as cooks or stewardesses. I had been lucky enough to secure jobs as a skipper, but never on boats that paid much money. The small amount of money I had succeeded in accumulating I was putting toward buying a small boat in Bequia, a small island, one of the Lesser Antilles in the Eastern Caribbean. I had arrived there delivering a boat for a friend. He had since run into serious problems with his export business back in Canada, leaving me with the responsibility of his boat. Bequia was a beautiful place to be stranded in.

It was a small island, only 7 square miles, but from the moment I arrived it felt like home. Sailing into Admiralty Bay for the first time was a shock; it was almost chock-a-block with more boats than I'd seen since leaving the United States. To our left, as we approached the small community that was Port Elizabeth, were white sandy beaches with lush foliage rising up behind and no large hotels or tourist buildings visible in any direction. The present-day Bequians were the direct descendants of the original native Carib Indians, escaped African slaves and early Scottish and Irish settlers; they were friendly, and the pace was relaxed and easy-going. The main visitors to the island were the numerous sun-baked sailors from all over the world. Both locals and visitors shared a long seafaring tradition that united them. Boats were still crafted by hand on the beaches, using tools and skills passed down from generation to generation.

I arrived there shortly before the launching of the 70-foot gaff schooner *Water Pearl* that Bob Dylan had commissioned and was being built on the beach in Admiralty Bay. For the launching, locals and visiting sailors hauled her into the water by hand, using methods unchanged over the centuries. Yes, indeed, Bequia was an easy place to be stranded in and to this day a part of my heart resides there in the lush green scenery, with the scent of frangipani and the sound of the steel drums.

Bequia

The summer of 1980 found me well traveled and happy but financially broke and living out of a single suitcase. As I sat gazing out to sea across Admiralty Bay, wondering what to do, I was approached with an offer to navigate an old three-masted schooner to Costa Rica.

"A quick trip under power, we just need you to show us the way," the owner's English upper-class accented voice boomed as smoke from his pipe wafted around me.

I needed the money and so I agreed, despite the fact that I would be alone with two old men, neither of whom knew anything about sailing. Inevitably the engine broke down, and I had to dig out sails, set them and basically single-handedly sail the boat. The ten-day trip ended up a month's voyage, and at the end the owner, who had jumped ship in Aruba, another Caribbean island that at the time formed a part of the Netherland Antilles, griped about paying me and only handed over what was agreed for ten days. So yet again, after an eventful trip, I had remarkably little money to show for it. I was sitting at a downtown bar in Puntarenas, the main port on Costa Rica's Pacific coast, where all the "gringos" from the yachts hung out. The bar was a lively place to meet people, hear news of friends, and find out what boats were going where and if there were any jobs. I drank a beer and chatted to a couple on their way north; we complained about yacht-owners and shared a few experiences before they had to leave. I noticed, as they left, a man sitting at the next table. He was tall with blond hair, an aquiline nose and penetrating blue eyes; probably ten to fifteen years older than me, clean-shaven and dressed smartly in a tailored linen suit. He smiled over at me:

"Seems like you had a pretty eventful trip?" He drawled in an American accent.

We sat and chatted. He managed to draw me out about my misgivings in having so little to show for all the years of hard work. Somehow, the conversation turned to drugs, and we discussed a mutual dislike for hard drugs but an enjoyment of marijuana and hashish:

"Think how much all our friends would appreciate the good

dope you find down here?"

"Yes, it's a shame we can't take it up to them."

"Well ... that's not exactly true, there's plenty that finds its way up to the US."

The conversation continued, not solely about drugs but somehow returned every now and then to the theme of smuggling. We laughed about the boats with their obviously drug-smuggling crews, three or four young men with no women, their boats not new but always with the latest, most expensive electronic equipment aboard. Jim, that was the name of my companion, pointed out that a woman, especially a woman skipper, would never be suspected. We were eating at this point and theorizing over a bottle of wine:

"It would be great to pick up offshore, and drop it off offshore, and never actually have to be in any country's territorial water. Just staying out at sea and not dealing with the legal risks."

It was fun fantasizing, and after the meal he wrote down a Florida phone number:

"Think about what I said and if you're interested call me."

I returned to Bequia, not much better off than when I'd left. The hurricane season was upon us, and I was planning to head south with the boat I was caretaking. I didn't get away in time, and Hurricane Alan, the first hurricane of the season, hit Bequia and put the boat on the beach. After I had her towed off and looked at the damage, I realized how much it would cost to repair and thought of Jim. The next day I called and told Jim I was thinking about his proposition. I had mentioned to him a boat named *Saada* that we could probably use as the owner had virtually abandoned her. At this moment she was anchored in Puntarenas, Costa Rica, but badly in need of repair. Jim was interested and told me to make contact with *Saada*'s owner. If he agreed to lend me the yacht, we would meet in Costa Rica. I did as he suggested and contacted the owner,

A LIFE AT SEA

Richard, an American businessman.

Two months later, as I flew into Miami to meet my connecting flight to San José, Costa Rica, I felt elated: the start of a new adventure, and this time I felt I would come out on top. As I waited for my San José flight, I bought a copy of a sailing magazine. In it was an inspiring article by Naomi James about single-handed sailing. "That's it!" I naively thought, "I'll do the trip alone, no worries about crew."

The bus from San José sped into Puntarenas. I got off by Pacifico Marine, a boatyard run by two American men; it was a small boatyard but they had all that was necessary for yacht repairs, and the two Americans did everything possible to help the passing boat people.

It was evening when I arrived, and there was no one there but the caretaker. I could see *Saada* anchored offshore, but the owner, Richard, who was supposed to be waiting for me with his dinghy, was nowhere to be seen. I asked the caretaker if he had seen anyone from *Saada*; he said he had seen someone waiting for maybe half an hour but then they had given up, so I sat there on the small dinghy pier waiting to catch a ride.

It was only a few months since I'd last been in Puntarenas but how differently I felt. It was a calm night with the light of a waxing moon shimmering over the boats anchored out in the river. I found myself gazing at the masts of *Saada* and smiled. She was a beautiful boat, and I had loved her when I first saw her eighteen months earlier in Golfito, a banana port, and further south down the coast close to the Panamanian border. At that time her main mast was broken off three feet from the deck, but the grace of her lines still made her memorable. She was an old Dutch-built steel boat, double-ended with a large beam – meaning rounded at both ends and very wide. She had a long history of neglect ever since she had come to the New World.

First she sat unused in Panama for many years and then the present owner bought her. He headed north on her but lost the main mast so had to leave her anchored mastless in Golfito for years. Earlier in 1980, he bought her a new mast and brought her to Puntarenas. He liked the image of himself as a sailor and boat owner, but in reality did little sailing and neglected his beautiful craft outrageously; he was always busy doing other things. Apparently he had been lucky in some property deals in southern California and Mexico and now had a few properties he rented out for a large profit. When I called him at his office from Bequia and offered to repair his boat if I could use her for a few months, he was delighted and not even interested in where I was going or why I should want to borrow her, seeing only that it would take the problem off his hands and cost him nothing.

I sat there gazing out at her, excited at the prospect of seeing her brightly painted and ready for sea after all these years. A few hours passed without me even noticing; I was just enjoying the peace and time alone. I knew that as soon as I stepped on board I would be working so hard it would be a long time before I could again sit so serenely. The quiet was suddenly disturbed by voices getting louder as they approached. Eventually they reached me: two men and a girl. As they went to get into their dinghy I asked them for a ride, and they gladly complied. We approached *Saada*, and they pulled alongside the rusty neglected yacht. I felt excited at the prospect of restoring her. Richard was aboard.

"Oh good, I was beginning to think you weren't coming and this was a wasted trip for me," he said with relief evident in his voice.

We talked for a short while before retiring to bed. Richard had, as I had asked him to, arranged for the boat to be taken to the boatyard for the initial repairs. The following morning we were due to be towed to the yard as the gears weren't working. The owners of the yard expected it to be a tough trip because of years of growth on *Saada*'s hull. After the long journey and the eventual excitement of finally being on *Saada*, I crawled through the chaos inside the boat to find the berth in the forecastle and slept soundly.

New sounds awoke me. A strong current ran down the river, and I could hear the water moving by the boat, so I got up. There was no water on board, which meant I could neither clean my teeth nor make a cup of tea; however, minutes after getting up, I heard the putt putt of an engine. It was the boat from the yard arriving to tow us in.

In my seven years of sailing I had been involved in countless boat haul-outs, but never had I seen or met the creatures that had taken up residence on *Saada*'s hull. Barnacles the size of tennis balls stared at me and at the sunlight disturbing their peaceful existence. If the hull had been made of anything else but steel, she would have sunk. The steel had rusted away in many places, especially around the deck. Parts of the hull were extremely thin and became holes after banging the rust away, so I marked them all ready for the welder. Richard was preparing to leave. He told me that urgent business meetings in Detroit meant he could devote no more time to helping me acquaint myself with *Saada*, but before he left he introduced me around the yard. I prepared myself for hard work, and I phoned Jim in Miami to let him know I had arrived and would need money immediately.

Saada was out of the water for a week, an intensive week, but both she and I needed it. The yard was friendly, and I had two men to help me. I also had the gearbox worked on. Richard had assured me that all the spars were new, as were both masts and their booms and the bowsprit; also that the rigging and the engine were in decent shape. I should never have taken his word without checking, but at that point I trusted his judgment and was overwhelmed with all I had to do. When the boat went back in the water, I started work on the deck, checking the mast fittings and clearing the interior. I only had one day off, which was when I went to San José to meet Jim and pick up money. It was the first time I'd seen him since our first meeting in Puntarenas, and it was interesting to see how things had changed: gone was the innocent fantasizing; now it was all business. He was exceedingly charming and good company, but he wanted everything ready as quickly as possible. He was staying in a beautiful hotel just outside the city, and I gratefully accepted his invitation to lunch in the panoramic restaurant. There, he expressed his concerns about my plan to do the trip alone:

"Two tons is a lot of marijuana to load and unload by yourself, you know?"

I suppose I'd only been thinking about the trip in terms of handling the boat, not the cargo:

"Well, we'll see," I said. "If I find someone, OK. But I can't think of anyone, and I'd rather be alone than have some idiot sail with me."

We arranged to meet in roughly ten days, at Balboa Yacht Club in Panama.

I had decided to stop off in Golfito. There I could remove all the superfluous equipment from the boat in order to leave room for my cargo and ask Captain Tom to watch it for me. Captain Tom was an American in his sixties who had run his boat up on the beach in Golfito thirty years previously and lived there ever since. He had a house and a bar on the beach and was host to all the visitors who passed through Golfito, as well as the locals. Golfito was a town I had enjoyed on previous visits, and Captain Tom was someone I always looked forward to seeing.

I spent a pleasant Thanksgiving evening with Bill and Ruby from Pacifico Marine, the main yacht marina, and two days later, on 29 November, I was ready to leave. The boat was seaworthy, but she still needed a lot of work, which I decided could be completed in Panama. The ensuing night the guys from the yard brought me the spinnaker pole that had been lying in the yard. I lifted my dinghy onto the deck, and first thing the next morning I motored down river to the fuel dock, filled my tanks and then motored out into the gulf. I was on my way.

The day was invigorating, and I loved the feeling I had of being alone on the boat – it was the greatest sensation of freedom. As I was heading across Gulfo Nicoya a breeze came up, so I went on the foredeck to pull up the sails. Five minutes later the wind had died, and the sails were slamming around. The Admiralty Pilot book (a sailor's bible) warns that the winds in this gulf are irregular, and the regularity of the currents cannot be depended upon; thus I spent a considerable amount of time putting sails up and pulling them down. My autopilot was one of the items I had decided to have repaired in Panama, so I was without any self-steering on this trip. Unfortunately if I left the helm under power she would go off in a big circle, so I had to stay at the helm, unable to cook nor even make a pot of coffee. None of that mattered as I felt marvelous and *Saada* enjoyed being on the move again.

Night started to fall and, as with every time I'd sailed in those waters, night-time brought with it an electrical storm of brilliant intensity. How small I felt in the face of such a formidable performance. So here I was on the first leg of my new adventure, soaking wet, hungry but ecstatic. I'd bought some amphetamines in Puntarenas before leaving as I knew there was no possibility of sleep on this phase of the trip; at around 1 a.m. I took my first, it worked fast and I felt fine.

The rain lasted most of the night, and morning dawned gray and cloudy, but it wasn't long before the sun broke through and dried everything off. For breakfast, starting to feel sleepy again, I took another pill and coffee, which I managed to make while tying the tiller off. I could see the rocks I needed to get past before heading into Gulfo Dulce; I was tired, but the joy of being out there sustained me. I turned into the gulf fairly early and was pleased to think I'd make it into Golfito before nightfall. I spent the day crossing the gulf and by four in the afternoon I could see the buildings of the town, when suddenly the afternoon rain descended upon me. It came down in thick sheets, and I could see nothing, my visibility suddenly being reduced to less than 30 feet. I sat offshore till it had passed, three-quarters of an hour later, and then headed into the bay. I had to take a pill every couple of hours now, but I kept telling myself that soon I could sleep.

There was still daylight as I came through the narrow passage into Golfito Bay and rounded the headland to anchor off Tom's beach. Memories flooded back of my first visit to Golfito. I felt the thrill of arriving somewhere by sea and thought of how pleased and surprised everyone would be to see me; luckily that gave me another spurt of energy. Dusk was falling and I slowed down, putting the engine into neutral and going forward to drop the anchor. Tired, and with my befuddled amphetamine brain, I dropped it before it dawned on me that I was still going forward. I returned to the cockpit and realized something was wrong with the gears: I was still in forward despite the lever being in neutral. I pulled at the gear lever and it went into reverse and stuck, so now I was heading backwards into the channel! I turned the engine off and moved toward the bow to pull the 40-pound anchor and 30 feet of chain back up.

"Well, I'd better try again if I'm going to get any sleep tonight," I said to myself, while going into the engine room to play with the gears. I managed to get them out of reverse but couldn't get them into neutral. I had to restart the engine in forward. This time I turned the engine off before dropping the anchor, but unfortunately after letting go of about 35 feet of chain, the links became twisted and stuck in the chain pipe. It was dark by now, and the cheerful lights at Tom's were twinkling across the water at me mockingly. I went down below to find a hammer to free the chain but realized I'd have to saw it. In the process of pulling enough chain back up to secure it around a cleat, I got my finger stuck under the chain. A pain shot through me and tears started rolling down my cheeks; I certainly didn't need this. I pulled my bruised finger clear and found a hacksaw with which I managed to saw through the chain either side of the pipe. Luckily there was another piece of pipe to use, and so I shackled the two parts of the chain together, and having checked in the chain locker that there were no more snags I prepared to pull the anchor up in preparation for another attempt at anchoring! As I drifted backwards and forwards, I thought how fortunate I was that at least there was no wind and only one other boat in the bay. I could feel the people on the other boat watching me and wondered tiredly and slightly irritatedly why they did not reach out and offer me assistance. Eventually my anchoring was successful. I went down below and saw it was 9.30 p.m. It had taken me three and a half hours to anchor. Should I have taken this as an omen of what the future had in store? No, I was too tired to think; I just looked at my bed and collapsed onto it

CHAPTER TWO

SNAKE ON BOARD

"I'm sure that's *Saada*." Charles McLean was sitting by the beach having a beer with Tom and his wife Rosia.

"No!" Tom answered unbelievingly. "It can't be ... but whoever it is, they seem to be having problems."

Soon they could no longer see the boat as night had fallen, just the running lights going backwards and forwards for three hours.

Charles sat there ruminating. He was a Scotsman of thirty-two, blond hair, blue eyes, bearded and 5 foot 9 inches tall. He'd been at sea since he was fifteen years old, first in the British Navy, followed by the Merchant Navy, and in the last few years on fishing boats and sailing boats, basically anything that could keep him afloat. Recently he'd been yearning for a long voyage; he was tired of spending too much time ashore, drinking too much and going nowhere. He looked out at *Saada*, a boat he knew well, remembering how much he had loved her and how bitter he still felt at how the owner, Richard, had used him. He wondered who would be on board this time.

The following morning I woke early and, still worrying about the gears, I went ashore. Rosia greeted me warmly, and as we talked Charles came wandering over. We'd met on a previous trip but hadn't gotten to know each other; he made a reference to having worked on *Saada* before, and how pleasant it was to see her in a better condition than when he had last seen her.

"Do you know anything about engines, or at least gearboxes?"

SNAKE ON BOARD

I asked him, and explained what had happened the night before. Charles smiled and said he had been watching and wondering what was up. He said he had sworn never to step on that boat again, but given it was me, he'd come out and look at it when he'd finished some painting he was doing for Tom. I waited ashore for him to finish, thankful for the rest. I looked out at *Saada* anchored peacefully in the bay and remembered how eighteen months earlier I'd sat in the same spot and watched her, at that time with a broken mast and a rusted hull. Beyond her lay the town of Golfito, with the main dock where the banana boats loaded up. Behind me and all around the bay hovered the lush green jungle. You could hear it constantly growing and felt if you ignored it for a while it would move in and take over.

Across the bay I saw a large rowing boat approaching; as it neared the shore I spotted Tom with one large paddle sculling, and I smiled. Tom was in his sixties, had lost one leg in the Guadalcanal campaign against the Japanese in 1943, but here he lived with his young family – he had found his Shangri-La. There was no road around to his beach from Golfito town, and it was a long way across the bay; he could have motored over, but Tom always rowed. He pulled the boat up onto the beach with the help of one of the local boys who helped him unload beer and supplies.

"Hi Tom," I said rising. He smiled, a knowing smile, not surprised to see me. He acted as if he knew I'd be there, although he hadn't recognized the shining gray boat anchored in the bay as *Saada*.

Around midday, Charles was ready to come out to the boat. It was Monday 1 December. On stepping aboard, he once again commented on how enjoyable it was to see her being cared for, as he too felt that she was too beautiful a boat to be left abandoned. He climbed down to the engine room, not knowing at that moment how many hours, days, weeks, months he was going to be spending

14

there. In fact, all of the problems stemmed from the same common cause, and that was rust. My troubles with the gears came from the fact that the screws holding the engine mounts in place had rusted away so that the whole engine was loose, and in addition, the mechanics in Puntarenas who had installed the gearbox had not tightened anything down. Charles spent the day with the engine and in the evening we sat and talked, enjoying each other's company.

He asked where I was taking the boat and, unable to look him in the eyes, I told Charles I was delivering the boat to the owner in Puerto Santos, Venezuela. Charles seemed surprised at this and said that when he knew Richard he had always been adamant about keeping the boat in San Francisco. He then related the story of his previous unpleasant experience with the owner of *Saada*. He had spent a few weeks working on the boat while the owner was away, but when Richard returned he accused Charles of stealing something and used that as an excuse not to pay him for his work. For a proud and stubborn Scot, the insult of being accused of theft was worse than not being paid.

I intended to spend only three or four days in Golfito, deciding I needed to be better prepared for the second leg of my trip to Panama. I had to fix things that had become apparent in the short trip from Puntarenas and would not make me reliant on amphetamines. I also had to take off all unnecessary equipment. I had asked Tom if he would mind storing some items for me, and he said, without asking questions, that it would be no problem. The three days seemed to go past quickly. I was spending all my time with Charles who unselfishly overhauled the engine and gearbox for me. We worked well together, enjoyed each other's company, and shared a love for *Saada*, despite Charles's contempt for the owner.

On the third day, when Charles was in the engine room and I was tidying up the main saloon, trying to work out what all the various wires were for, I suddenly saw a wire move. I jumped as I realized it was a snake about 5 feet long with beady eyes in a diamond-shaped head staring at me.

"Charles, Charles, there's a snake looking at me." Charles banged his head as he looked up at me in disbelief. "It's true," I continued, in a shaky voice, "come and see." He climbed out of the engine room and looked across the main saloon at it, now coiling itself around the light fitting. Picking up a barbecue fork he quickly attached it to a pole and slowly moved toward the snake. The snake saw him coming and it too moved toward Charles, flicking its tongue viciously. We both beat a hasty retreat to the cockpit. What should we do now? Where did it come from and, more to the point, how were we going to get rid of it?

"Let's go and ask Tom," Charles suggested. Thus, grateful to have an excuse to escape, we rowed ashore. Tom, his face creased with laughter, suggested shooting it. "We can't start shooting holes all over the boat," I argued.

"Well maybe one good shot, if it's not below the water line," Tom countered. Where to get a gun became the next problem. "Why not try the other boat in the bay?" offered Tom. We rowed over to them. It was the boat that had watched me arrive the first night but had done nothing to help; I did not have friendly feelings toward them. As we came alongside I called to them, and finally a nervous-looking brown-haired woman, aged about fifty-five, appeared. "Yes," she said in a Canadian accent, "what do you want?"

"We want to borrow a gun," Charles answered. What an opening! The woman's eyes widened with fear, so I hurriedly explained the situation to her. She calmed down and elucidated her own story; it seemed they had been victims of piracy in Colombian waters. Piracy against private yachts often remains completely unreported. Robbers armed with guns and knives had boarded their 49-foot yacht anchored overnight about 30 miles south off

SAILING INTO THE ABYSS

Cartagena, in a bay off the Baru peninsula; the robbers had tied up her husband and 20-year-old son and stolen the ship's stores and other valuables. Though escaping with their lives, they had been badly affected by the whole experience and simply wished to return to Canada as quickly as they could. Fear coursed up my spine as I realized the waters where the pirates had attacked them were the same seas that I would be navigating single-handed. Their dream of a carefree life of retirement, going where they wished when they wanted, had been shattered. They did have a gun, but she couldn't let us have it without her husband's permission, and he had gone to town with their son.

Charles had another idea: "Jorge's good with snakes, we'll go and ask him." It turned out that Jorge was a local teenager known for both his knowledge of snakes and his ability to catch or kill them; an important skill in a country where the vast majority of snakes are highly poisonous. Jorge lived on the same beach as Tom, so we quickly found him and he rowed back to the boat with us. We were hoping the snake hadn't disappeared behind the paneling or into the bilges. Luckily, as we looked into the main saloon, we saw the tip of its tail hanging out from inside a cabinet. Jorge, although not tall, was dark and lean with bright, sparkling eyes; he moved stealthily across the cabin and quickly took the end of the tail in his right hand and started to pull the snake backwards. He kept his left hand on the cabinet door, and as he neared the head he pulled it open and quick as lightning he smashed it back on the snake's head, stunning it. He then brought it out and observed it. It was not, in fact, poisonous though it closely resembled a deadly poisonous one. He threw it in the dinghy, and we all rowed ashore. I looked at it and started trembling. I'd gone to sea prepared to deal with storms, unknown coasts and boat problems, but not snakes. The thought that I'd been living alone with a snake suddenly hit me and I couldn't stop shaking.

SNAKE ON BOARD

That evening Charles took me to his hut on the edge of the jungle and cooked me a shark steak on the barbecue in an attempt to calm me down. Charles and I worked out that the snake must have crept inside the spinnaker pole whilst it lay unattended in the boat yard in Puntarenas and was brought aboard the night before I left Puntarenas. I was relieved it hadn't decided to introduce itself whilst I was out on the open ocean.

After dinner we lay on the beach, and it only seemed natural for me to seek comfort in his arms. Before long this led to our lips seeking each other's and, with passion ignited, we hungrily devoured each other's body. It felt right and so agreeable. As dawn broke, and with our bodies saturated with love, I confided to Charles what my journey was actually about. When I had finished my ramble Charles remained silent. I began to think I had seriously blown it, and then, unexpectedly, Charles began to laugh.

"My god," he said, "you are one hell of a crazy chick. But if you think I'm going to let you do it on your own, you can think again. I'm coming with you."

I lay in stunned silence. I had by now had the idea firmly entrenched in my mind that I was doing the trip on my own. I wanted to do it on my own. I thought back to the article I had read in the airport in Miami of Naomi James sailing single-handed, and the amazing accomplishment she must have felt. But then I thought of the fear, and the tiredness I had felt when the gearing had broken on me. I also realized that I thoroughly enjoyed the closeness Charles and I had established, and I didn't want to lose that; and practically, having him along to help with the engine and the cargo made a lot of sense. After hearing of the pirate attack from the Canadian woman that afternoon I suddenly felt an immense sense of relief. I sat up and looked at him.

"Do you seriously mean that?" I asked.

"Well, do you really think I could ever get peaceful night's sleep again thinking of you undertaking such a dangerous voyage on your own?"

He sat up and lit a cigarette, and turned to look at me, stroking the hair from my face.

"Besides," he said, "I've been too long on land and need some adventure."

The following morning we had breakfast at Tom and Rosito's and Charles announced to them that he was joining me aboard *Saada*. Tom and Rosito exchanged knowing glances and I felt myself blushing. They were overjoyed, as they had worried about me doing the journey alone and also realized that Charles needed to leave.

To everyone in Golfito we said we were delivering the boat for the owner to Puerto Santos, in Venezuela. Everyone accepted this, as it was not an unusual scenario in the boating world. Boat owners were busy people earning money through their various businesses, and if they wanted their yacht to be in another place for a vacation they would pay someone to deliver it for them.

Charles and I decided to leave the following evening to catch the most favorable current through the gulf. Having made up his mind to join me, Charles quickly got into the preparations, from going up the mast to checking the rigging and making final checks on the engine. The following afternoon at five Charles said "Goodbye" and "See you soon" to all his friends, then joined me on board. I pulled up the anchor and we motored out of the bay on *Saada*, who was ready for the next leg of her adventure.

The normal time for the trip from Golfito to Panama is three to four days; it took us seven days and made me thankful and joyous that Charles was with me. The journey was useful as it showed up the numerous things that still needed to be repaired on the boat, and it also gave the three of us time to get to know each other. We could feel Saada begin to come to life, and when we had wind and were heading south she flew with joy over the waves. The offshore winds between Golfito and the Gulf of Panama are variable in direction and velocity and interrupted by calms and ocean squalls, so this was also the beginning of our relationship with the motor. Our major engine problem on this part of the trip was overheating caused by a clogged water pump. We could only run it at low revs and for a couple of hours at a time. This meant that, in periods of no wind, we would motor along at 2-3 knots, little realizing that this would be our average speed on the trip north after picking up our cargo. The sun was shining, the days were warm and we had plenty to talk about; and there was a great deal to look at, so we were not too disturbed at our slow progress. We passed offshore islands such as Isla Coiba and Isla Jicaron. Isla Coiba had a penal colony on its east side, and we thought of the poor prisoners trapped, never considering that we could ever be prisoners ourselves. The west side is mountainous and lush and looked beautiful in the morning sun. We saw turtles, sharks and dolphins; the Pacific Ocean is very alive and we were reveling in being a part of it.

There was no sextant on board (the instrument used to measure the angle between a celestial body and the horizon to pinpoint your position), so we were dependent on our dead reckoning calculations, and with the bizarre currents prevalent in those waters we couldn't always be certain of them; especially when we had lost sight of land. We had been reaching (when the boat is traveling approximately perpendicular to the wind) for a few hours now. The wind was blowing from the north-east onto our beam, and *Saada* raced through the water with delight. It seemed she would just go on forever, and we both felt the same elation; but eventually we reckoned we should head into the Bay of Panama, which was after all our first destination. As we pulled in our sheets to head her in a northerly direction, *Saada* seemed suddenly to sense where we were heading and refused to go. The seas were not particularly large nor the wind that strong, but all of a sudden we had a boat flinging itself from side to side and up and down, throwing everything below into disarray and confusing us totally. This display lasted for the next twelve hours without ceasing, even when the wind dropped entirely and we were under power. It took us three days to pass the 100 miles across the Gulf of Panama: three days of forcing an unwilling boat to return to the place where she'd lain neglected for so long. We told her that soon she'd be going on a long, long journey and that we'd never neglect her, but the togetherness we'd felt and the trust we'd sensed had disappeared. Having no sextant and unnerved by the seemingly inexplicable behavior of our boat, it was difficult to know exactly where we were, especially as we saw so few other boats, even though we knew there were many big ships out there somewhere headed for the canal.

Eventually we began to see ships and then lights and the vague outline of land. We passed by Taboga Island and approached the beginning of the canal. Exhausted, we dropped our anchor off the lighthouse on Flamenco Island, making sure both our quarantine flag and Panamanian flag were hoisted, to show the Panamanian authorities we were entering their country. It wasn't until the Immigration vessel was pulling up alongside our boat that Charles announced he had no passport. He had lost it a few months earlier and hadn't even thought of it when we were leaving Costa Rica. Charles had previously lived in Panama and luckily had on him his out-of-date Panama *residencia*, which at least proved his identity and enabled us to enter Panama. Nonetheless, we were told we were to visit Immigration dock 11 the following day.

After we were cleared we motored on down toward the canal, and just before we passed under the Bridge of the Americas we tied up to a mooring at the Balboa Yacht Club. This yacht club in 1980 was a large wooden building sitting right next to the Pacific entrance to the Panama Canal. It was a well-known landmark to boaters from around the world, and a place where you could find line-handlers to get through the canal, a mechanic to get something fixed, anchorage for your boat while you got a bite to eat; it had served as the entry point to the country of Panama for many people for years. It was a magical place, as you could watch the endless stream of boats going from the Pacific to the Atlantic, and from the Atlantic to the Pacific; and you could see the cars crossing the bridge from North America to South America and from South America to North America – the crossroads of the world. Since that time, the old wooden building has burned down.

At the time we were there in 1980, there was only one dock, the fuel dock. All the boats tied up to moorings, and then one of the two yacht club launches picked you up when you needed to go ashore. We were tied to an outside buoy, having the advantage of the movie-like procession of ships heading in and out of the canal, but the disadvantage of being a fair distance from the launch dock and therefore having to wait a long time to get ashore.

It was 4 p.m. on Wednesday 10 December when we finally tied up to our buoy, and we were anxious to get ashore to have a shower, drink a cold beer, make contact with Jim, and be out of Panama as quickly as possible. Amazingly we achieved the first three objectives within an hour. I found out that Jim had been waiting for me a few days earlier but had then given up and returned to the United States; luckily he had just arrived back in Panama City. I contacted him at the Hilton and was soon in a taxi cab to go and meet him. One of the joys of sailing is to be out at sea having few facilities and no luxuries, and then to come into land and enjoy civilization again. It makes one appreciate the best of both worlds. Within a couple of hours, having showered and changed from sailing gear into a dress, I was sipping a cocktail at the Hilton and following it with a Japanese meal. Jim had with him his pretty young blonde girlfriend, Sally, and we shared an enjoyable evening. I filled him in on our voyage and the problems with the boat. He was relieved to hear about Charles, as he had always worried about me tackling the trip alone. He had even gone as far as approaching a possible crew member himself during his visits to the yacht club. The only dampener on the evening was receiving the news that John Lennon had been shot dead two days earlier in New York while we were crossing the Bay of Panama.

Jim and Sally said they'd be down to see the boat in a few days, and Jim would bring me the electronic equipment he had ordered for me. I returned to *Saada* where Charles was already asleep. I crawled into bed beside him and woke him to talk excitedly about my evening with Jim and Sally. Full of positive energy, we made love before falling into a deeply relaxed sleep.

CHAPTER THREE

THE ADVENTURE BEGINS

Panama City is a large bustling international city. When Charles and I were there in 1980, the population was about 430,000 people. Balboa was the American section of Panama City until 1 October 1979. The Panamanians then regained control of the 533 square miles of Canal Zone, though allowing the United States to continue operating the canal itself. The American Legion, despite being open to Panamanians, tended to be a little American enclave where, like British colonies in India and French colonies in North Africa, the Americans lived in an isolated small world about ten years behind the times.

When Charles and I pulled into Balboa, we expected to be there for a week. We had repairs to make, both on the boat and the engine, and we had to install all our newly bought electronic equipment that Jim had supplied. We also had to meet with Jim's Colombian contacts, to coordinate our plans for picking up our cargo. On Thursday morning, the day after our arrival, Charles went down into the engine room while I attacked the long list of things to do and made the first of many trips into Panama City. We were facing roughly two months at sea so would need a lot of supplies, and we would have the added difficulty of having limited space to store these supplies. *Saada* was a wide boat. You went from the cockpit into an area about 3 feet square down some steps. To the right was the navigation area and to the left the cooker and sink.

SAILING INTO THE ABYSS

From here you went down another step into the main saloon. Forward of the main saloon were two small cubicles facing each other: one was the toilet and shower and the other the hanging locker. Forward again was the forecastle with two berths. Two tons of marijuana were going to occupy virtually all the main saloon, the forecastle, the toilet and hanging locker, leaving us only the area between the cooker and navigation table in which to exist and store everything. We would have to sleep on top of the bales of marijuana!

I had to find a wet/dry vacuum and other things to clean the boat after the marijuana was offloaded. We needed numerous plastic bags to pack the marijuana, as the Colombians would probably not have it packed as well as was necessary for a long ocean passage. Of course, we also had to get all our food, medical supplies and navigational equipment. All our water would have to be carried on deck, as our water tanks were rusted beyond repair. There was netting for the bowsprit to be found, as the bow pulpit had been damaged and never replaced, making some of the head sail changes dangerous. I wanted a frame for the cooker to secure pots and pans as, though gimbaled, in a heavy sea a hot pot of coffee could easily go flying. The sails left for years on the spars were not as good as new: the stitching had rotted away in many places, so not only did I need a dependable sail repair kit, but we were also looking for a new head sail. We needed charts. We needed hardware, such as blocks and shackles. There was a separate list of things needed for the engine. We also needed a new battery and spares for everything.

In a United States port such as San Diego or San Francisco, or in England, all this would not be too difficult to accomplish; but in Panama at the time it did not cater so well for cruising yachts. If I couldn't find things, I had to find somewhere to make them. Every relevant shop or work place was in a different part of the city, thus finding everything was extremely time-consuming. Charles and I started work early each morning and in the evenings stopped for a couple of drinks in the yacht club before going back to the boat. We liked to sit out in the cockpit and watch the ships from all over the world go to and from the canal.

On our second evening, the crew member discovered by Jim turned up in the yacht club. His name was Tony, but we christened him "Good Vibes" as Jim had admitted he had no sailing experience but did have good vibes. I took him out to see *Saada* and talk to him.

"Yea, well, I'd like to do the trip but I need to be in California early in January to go skiing, so what day do you think we'll be there?" I tried to answer him by explaining that on the voyage we were about to undertake one could not give a date, as we would be going against wind and current.

"Do you know anything about engines?" I asked him. "Nothing at all," he said proudly. "If anything goes wrong with my car I get it towed to the nearest mechanic." Charles went on deck to fetch water and took Tony who was horrified. "You mean you can't just turn on a tap?" The encounter had simply reinforced my newly discovered need for Charles, and I realized that even if he had not offered to join me, nothing would have induced me to go to sea with an inexperienced person like Tony; you need more than good vibes out on the ocean.

Jim and Sally came to visit the boat. They were shocked by how much needed doing; I was glad Jim had not seen her before the yard in Puntarenas.

"You'll probably take at least two weeks to get ready," he commented.

"No," I said, "we're working extremely hard and could be ready in a week. That's assuming the radio equipment isn't a problem, but I've already found a company to install that."

"Well ..." Jim paused, looking at Sally. It was difficult to read what his expression meant. "Why not plan to leave at the beginning of January? That way you can enjoy Christmas here. The Colombians could probably use a couple more weeks, but anyway, we'll be back before Christmas to set up a final meeting with Manuel."

I had met Manuel the afternoon before, a meeting arranged in the Holiday Inn. He was a pleasant man, stockily built, and smartly dressed in a gray suit; he reminded me of my father's business associates I'd met as a child, though, I hasten to add, they were not drug dealers. Manuel had shown me the general area where we would be rendezvousing with his people, but for some reason we had not finalized anything.

Charles was not too happy with the delay. He didn't like to be around lots of people and hated cities; in fact, apart from the necessary trips to the British Embassy and the Panamanian Immigration office about his passport, I couldn't get him into Panama City. He did, however, realize that we could do with the extra time to get *Saada* ready for the trip, so we settled into a three-week stay in Panama.

One of the problems at Balboa Yacht Club was that we could only afford to stay a week at a time; after one week the rates, already high, continually increased. Thus, we did the same as the other cruising boats and sailed over to Taboga.

Taboga is a truly beautiful island, roughly ten miles from Panama City. There are ferries daily between Panama City and Taboga. Before sailing there, we had our electronic gear installed. Jim had got us a Loran, a navigational aid that would give us our position but only when we were close to United States waters. We had a VHF radio with a direction-finding antenna. A VHF radio only communicates over a short distance; the direction-finding antenna was to enable us to pinpoint the position of the rendezvous boat when we made contact. For long-range communication we had a ham radio with attendant tuner. It was a compact little set that picked up all shortwave stations; the BBC was to provide hours of entertainment. We kept close contact with Jim and his associates, the only problem being that the ability to make contact was affected by weather conditions. Along with the radios came two large bladders: a 100 gallon one and a 50 gallon one. We called them our whales, intending to use the larger one for water and the smaller one for fuel; they were big black rubber containers which we had to secure somehow to the decks and then work out how to get the relevant liquid from them.

The other significant time consumer, that first week, was the hours spent in the downtown immigration office. The British Embassy said there would be no problem getting Charles a new passport as he had reported its loss to their office in Costa Rica. They said he could have his new one within three days. Unfortunately it didn't go quite that smoothly with the Panamanian Immigration. We had been sent to the downtown office from Immigration Dock II. Luckily Charles's Panamanian residence card, though out of date, helped establish his identity and probably saved him from either detention or deportation. While we were sitting there, we saw them handcuff someone in an adjoining room. A cold sweat came over me at the thought of someone losing their freedom. The Immigration officer wanted to see Charles's new passport as soon as he got it, so when a couple of days later I picked up the passport I took it straight there. I was horrified when they took it. It seemed an arbitrary act. I saw the wrong official at the wrong time; he needed to assert some authority to make himself feel better, and I arrived at that point. Each trip to the Immigration office took at least three hours, so we were facing at least one more visit before we left and a possible fine.

Our first week rushed by in a flurry of activity. A few boats had arrived that Charles had recognized from Golfito, cruising couples on their way to the South Pacific, and as they had all moved to Taboga we were not too depressed at the thought of spending Christmas there. Sailing over we found about eight yachts anchored in the bay. We anchored close to *Maverick*, a pretty green ketch belonging to a young couple, Max and Vera Zenobi. They were to become close friends during our stay there, though it was always difficult to have to lie to such considerate friends as to what and where we were going. Max was a ham operator, an electronic genius who could talk for hours on the subject and taught us a terrific amount about our radio and other equipment. The other cruising boats in Taboga over Christmas belonged to older couples whose children had grown up, and they had exchanged their homes for boats and just taken off. They all had different stories, and all were interesting people. We were invited to share Christmas dinner on one of the boats, five boats getting together and each contributing something toward the meal. I made the roast potatoes and chestnut stuffing for the turkey.

Christmas Day dawned, the heat already overwhelming; I never quite got used to a hot Christmas Day. Charles was used to spending Christmas at sea, whereas I came from a large family and it was a hugely important day. In one of my trips over to Panama City, I had picked up a Buck knife as a present for Charles. He was so genuinely surprised that it was a treat for me to give it to him. We did a couple of hours' work in the morning and took the rest of the day off: our first day off since starting this journey. It was an enjoyable day spent with pleasant people who all assumed we were another cruising couple. Jim was right, no one suspected us even with our new electronic gear, so significant to us, but not much different than the equipment carried by the other boats.

Jim and Sally did not appear before Christmas, but we had set up a radio schedule. The first couple of days I couldn't reach them, but then on the third day I made contact. It was difficult to talk because of heavy traffic, so we tried a quieter frequency. Jim told me to meet Manuel on 26 December at the Holiday Inn; so the day after Christmas we sailed back to Balboa early and I excitedly set off to meet him.

I enjoyed Panama City, the colors, the enthusiasm, the buses each individually painted with bright gold, red and blue depicting radiant scenes, mainly religious, and blaring loud music, and the street vendors cheerfully shouting out the virtues of their wares. I smiled at it all, pleased to have been part of it, but glad to be leaving soon.

"I want to know what room Manuel Rodriguez is in, please." I waited by the reception desk in the Holiday Inn while they checked the register.

"I'm sorry, we have no one registered in that name."

Disappointment hit me. I should have phoned before leaving the yacht club. Maybe he was staying at the Hilton instead. I phoned but already knew the answer, he wasn't there. I tried to contact Jim, but he wasn't available either; however, someone was who gave me a number in Medellin, Colombia, to call. Finally, I managed to talk to Manuel. In the background it sounded as if a large party was going on. Manuel was surprised to hear I expected to see him. "It's Christmas. I can't leave my family at this time. I'll see you in about two weeks. I'll let Jim know when."

I was afraid to tell Charles. He was happier in Taboga than Panama City, but still wanted to get going; Max and Vera had bid us farewell. They were heading to the Perlas Islands, a group of islands situated in the Bay of Panama. When I told Charles of the additional delay, we decided to return to Taboga and sail with them. We set sail early on 27 December, a beautiful day, a beautiful sail. *Saada* was again in her element. We fished on the way; trolling a line we caught a couple of tuna and four Bonita. When we sailed into the archipelago and anchored in the Bay of Contadora Island, we forgot

SAILING INTO THE ABYSS

Jim and Manuel and got together with the other boats to cook up the fish.

Contadina is an exquisite island with white beaches and clear blue water. The Shah of Iran lived there for a time, and I could understand why anyone with money would live there when only fifteen minutes away by air is Panama City with its large commercial and banking center and its international airport. We strolled up to the hotel and swam in their pool, the first pool I'd seen with the bar situated in the pool, so you swam up for your drinks and sat on seats that were underwater. As we sat there enjoying our holiday, Charles and I decided that when all was over we would have a brief holiday there together, before carrying on with our lives. The few days we spent there gave us the energy to deal with Panama City yet again.

Jim and Sally were flying in on 2 January, so we phoned the yacht club to ensure a mooring and on 31 December we set off to sail back once more to Panama City. Yet again *Saada* fought the trip back to Panama, not as dramatically as the first time, but her distaste for returning to Balboa remained evident. We had a fair wind on the way back and had to beat into it so were able to see how *Saada* did against the wind. She sailed beautifully, if unwillingly, the only serious mishap being the shackle on the main sheet breaking without warning causing momentary chaos. I'd never been on a boat where things collapsed with such regularity. Maybe I should have taken it as a warning.

At about 6 o'clock on New Year's Eve, we were again secured to a mooring at the yacht club. We heard the New Year's Eve celebration starting ashore and knew there would be a lot of very drunken revelers. We didn't feel like being with a crowd, so had an early night.

Jim and Sally did not come down to the boat, so I went to meet them. They took me out to dinner, always enjoyable as Charles and I couldn't afford to eat out. They had brought me a sextant as I hadn't managed to find one in Panama. Manuel had set up another meeting for Wednesday 14 January, so Jim thought the sensible thing for us to do was to return to the Perlas and just relax. The boat was fully prepared now, and the final stocking up couldn't be done until we were ready to leave.

"So you might as well go and return mid January."

It's true that this seemed the sensible thing to do, so a couple of days later we headed back to the Perlas. I had new radio schedules to try out and was still learning more and more from Max. Charles was still working through the engine, something new breaking each time we used it.

Life was enjoyable in the Perlas, but the waiting was hard as were the lies we had to tell to friends. The original story of a delivery seemed strange when we hung around for weeks. Also, money was tight. In the early days Jim was extremely generous but had gotten less so as time went on, so we ate simply aboard, having the occasional beer ashore. The local marijuana in Panama was exceptionally good and remarkably cheap. I would bake cakes, and we would eat it or smoke it, go for walks, swim and dive. It fitted in with the mellow life style of both the islanders and the boat people. It also kept us in the mood for our enterprise as we enjoyed being with people who smoked marijuana, as opposed to the raucous heavy drinking that went on in the Balboa Yacht Club. We sailed around the other islands in the Archipelago: Isla del Rey, Isla San José, each one different but all lush, green and unspoilt. It was difficult to relax knowing the voyage that lay ahead. We wished we were enjoying everything here after a successful trip, and talked about heading straight back after off loading our cargo, not bothering to go to the United States at all.

Tuesday 13 January saw us heading yet again to Panama City. There was no room in Balboa for a day, so we tried anchoring off the main beach, this being the only other place to anchor off Panama City. I went ashore to make contact, not that easy an operation, as we had to anchor so far offshore that we needed to pay a small boat to come and pick me up. Charles stayed with the boat feeling majorly exposed. Yet again Manuel was not there and yet again I phoned Medellin. Manuel was hugely apologetic but evasive, giving me no clear answers, so I tried unsuccessfully to contact Jim. Returning to the boat I tried to sound more positive than I felt to Charles, who had been dealing with the anchor dragging as the tide came in. We managed an uncomfortable night and returned to Taboga the next day, having been promised a mooring the following day by the yacht club. We returned to Balboa feeling an empathy with *Saada*; we also felt we'd had enough of Panama City. We tied up and went ashore to persist in our efforts to reach Jim.

Charles was beginning to lose hope of the voyage ever happening and wondered why he'd ever left Golfito. We were arguing a lot and drinking too much. I listened to my radio schedule daily but got no response from that either. Finally, we got hold of Jim who said he'd be down in a week. It was back again to Taboga and then a return to Balboa to see him. We were spending more time in the yacht club now, drinking and joining in happy hours and weekly dances. We were leading a life totally opposite to the one we hoped to be leading very soon, picking up the spirit of a world in limbo. The Americans living in the Canal Zone were still coming to terms with the canal having been handed over the previous October to the Panamanians. Many of them were bitter, most of them uncertain.

Jim showed up. Apparently the problems stemmed from money. The cargo was not being paid for upfront, but the pilot who was flying it from the interior of Colombia to the West Coast wanted to be paid and Manuel and Jim could not decide who should pay him. He said Manuel was coming in at the beginning of February, and they should be able to sort it out. Thus, we were off to Taboga again, back to the lies and back to the bar. Charles was skeptical of Manuel arriving in February, but he did. We finally spent the day planning, as we'd waited to do for two months. We set up a meeting date of 23 February, one hundred miles off the Colombian coast, due west of Cabo Corrientes. We shook hands and left: at last things were happening. We still had two weeks so made a final work list, took what was necessary and headed back out to the Perlas. We particularly enjoyed this trip as we knew it was our last. Days passed easily: doing some work on the boat, fishing and then salting the fish for the trip, and marinating it to make fish jerky. Charles was going out on a hobie cat every day, and even ran accidentally over the back of a whale. We helped friends haul out their boats on the sheltered beaches, and we met boats from the Caribbean on their way to the South Pacific, many of whom I recognized from my days in Bequia.

Finally, we came back to Panama City for one last time to stock up. We had a contact who took us to the PX, the shop on the US Army base, where food was duty free so considerably cheaper than in the town. We filled a taxi full of food and storing tins, bought a case of soda, a case of ginger ale, a bottle of rum for the occasional evening cocktail and finally a bottle of Dom Pérignon champagne in anticipation of celebrating the end of the trip. Back on the boat, I oiled one hundred and twenty eggs, hung vegetables and sorted out books to read.

We still needed to collect Charles's passport from Immigration. We dreaded the trip to the gray military-looking building in downtown Panama City. We entered and queued up at the first desk in order to start the bureaucratic ball rolling. After about two hours, we saw the official who had taken Charles's passport. Instead of giving us his passport they wanted to see mine. Reluctantly I handed it to him, and he looked through it. Looking up at me, his small moustache and piercing eyes suddenly making him look like Hitler, he told us to return the next day. With that, he turned and crisply strode off taking my passport with him. That ruined our day, and we spent a worried evening in the yacht club. We listened to assorted immigration stories from other boat people; one couple had been made to pay $200 for not having a particular stamp. We returned early the next day and spent another frustrating three hours. All of a sudden the same official who had given us so much trouble returned smiling and handed Charles his passport. At the same time he handed me a slip of paper saying I had to pay a $12 fine for the return of my passport. I didn't understand why but was not going to argue, so I paid the fee, took my passport and thankfully we left.

The boat was fully stocked now, so we cleared out of Panama, went to the fuel dock and filled up with fuel and water. At 7 o'clock we motored over to Taboga for the evening. Everyone was waiting for us, ready to bid us on our way. The next day, 21 February 1981, the sun rose as we pulled up the anchor and off we went; the three of us, elated and smiling; no more trips to Panama City.

Finally, our adventure was beginning.

CHAPTER FOUR

MARIJUANA GALORE

The sea was glassy, the sky cloudless. We motored away from Taboga under a glowing sun, the blares of our friends' horns fading in the distance. "Finally off," Charles smiled to himself and at me, "though I'll feel better when we're loaded up and headed north."

"Yes," I agreed, equally relieved to be off, but already wondering about the next stage. Would it be calm enough to raft up with the other boat? Would they transport it by dinghy? Within the hour a small breeze had sprung up from the north, and as we pulled up the sails and turned off the engine I forgot all about any problems there might be ahead. I settled into the pleasure of *Saada* moving through the water under sail, leaving the land behind and heading south, the headsail poled out pulling us on. We set the self-steering and had a celebration can of beer, put out the fishing line and just reveled in the morning.

We did have quite a few things still left to do before meeting the Colombians. We had to put the storm ports over the portholes, clear out down below, neither of which we could do before without making our friends suspicious. Our wet/dry vacuum was hidden and could remain so as we wouldn't need it till the cargo had been taken off. There was no hurry. We weren't expecting to be close to our rendezvous point until very early on the morning of 23 February 1981. In fact with fair winds we were there around midnight the night before. We were about one hundred miles off the Colombian coast and luckily it was a calm night, so we just turned off the motor and switched on the VHF and sat there.

"Marie-Louise, Marie-Louise, aqui esta, Ave del Mar."

We jumped. It was the code names chosen for the boats. They were here! It was finally happening. We answered and quickly changed channels. There on the screen was a signal; the radio direction antenna was working. We headed for it. It took us two hours till we saw a light, and within another hour we could see them, a fishing boat about 60 feet long. She was brightly lit, a scruffy-looking boat, and we could see four or five men looking at us. We motored close to them, and the Captain signaled to us. He didn't want us to come alongside as, though it was a windless night, there was still enough of a swell to make rafting up together a problem. They had two dinghies visible. They threw us a line, and we hung off their stern. The two dinghies using the line to pull backwards came either side of us. In each dinghy were two men and about ten bales of marijuana. One man from each dinghy came aboard. They were young, grinning wildly, showing a mouth full of broken and gold teeth. They greeted us amicably, introducing themselves as Gonzales and Pedro. We established they were going to help us load the boat.

We greatly appreciated their help. They were obviously delighted with their work, and they looked around *Saada* with some amusement.

"This go to United State?" they asked wonderingly.

"How long?" Pedro wanted to know, when Charles had assured them she would sail to the US.

When we told them, they looked at each other in amazement. We started to load the marijuana. It amused them that I was working, but they treated me with ample respect. Charles and Pedro went down below and started piling it in while Gonzales and I passed it down to them. There was a terrific feeling of camaraderie.

MARIJUANA GALORE

They had brought us some cold beer and I gave them some cookies and cakes. We could hear the men in the fishing boat, jovial noises and the hum of the engines. At one point I looked up: the sky was black and the waning moon that had come up around 11 p.m., two days after full, was glowing orange and riding high in the sky; Sirius was sparkling, the water was gleaming silver in the moonlight, the yellow lights of the fishing boat up ahead were twinkling and the laughter of the men was dancing across the water. A large smile and warm feeling spread all over me; I would never forget this night. There was so much warm feeling between the participants and so much magic in the air.

Pedro couldn't handle being down below piling up any more blocks of marijuana as the fumes were overwhelming, so he changed places with Gonzales. Just as day broke we finished and, casting off the line connecting us, we bid farewell to our companions of one night. They wished us heartfelt luck as their payment like ours probably depended upon the success of our trip.

Finally we were off, the land forgotten, and we settled into the life we both loved so much out on the ocean. We looked into the boat and saw that the marijuana covered everything. We had left approximately 30 inches above the central area, so we could crawl through to the forecastle, sleep on top and get to the seacock or anchor if necessary. We needed some rest before the job of repacking the bales, so set the wind vane, and as I took the first watch, Charles went to get some sleep.

We organized our watches as three hours on, three hours off through twenty-four hours. At night, the person coming off watch made sure there was fresh coffee for the person coming on watch. I tended to do most of the cooking and Charles the engine work. We were both capable of doing the other, which we did whenever the other was burned out with a particular job. Ingeniously I had stored everything for two months at sea into a tiny area, which meant that when Charles cooked he had to ask continually where everything was. The navigation, however, we shared, each taking sights when we were awake. Charles took the better sun sights and I liked shooting the stars and planets. Before the end of the trip we were so in tune with the stars, we used them to tell the time. Where else but at sea do you get to sit outside, gazing at the sky all your waking hours?

Only four times did we get verification of our sights and each time we were delighted to be spot on. The first time was close to Clipperton Island, an uninhabited 3.5 square-mile coral atoll in the eastern Pacific Ocean, south-west of Mexico and west of Central America. We spotted a tuna boat and called them on VHF; luckily, as maybe a half hour later a helicopter came cruising by us, waving and smiling. We would have been extremely nervous if we hadn't talked to the tuna boat who had mentioned the helicopter. The next time was when we were a week overdue meeting our rendezvous boat and we saw the light of a ship in the distance. It was a British ship, and we chatted for maybe fifteen minutes on and off on the radio. Four weeks later, when desperate for water, we saw a large tanker. We hinted strongly about our lack of water, but they just told us there was a rain shower on the way and confirmed our position. We saw the rain shower but never got to it in time. Finally, when our Loran began to make sense, we were exactly where we had calculated. We quickly settled into a routine. It took a couple of days to repack all the bales, as moving them about and getting to the ones in the fo'c'sle was hard. When that was finished, we just concentrated on sailing north. We listened to the radio twice a day, once in the morning and once in the afternoon. We had a list of names to represent each five degrees of latitude, and we would include the relevant name in the conversation, thus conveying our position. There were two possible rendezvous points we had arranged with Jim: Brenda, 300 miles off San Diego; and Angela,

MARIJUANA GALORE

300 miles off San Francisco. We were to be told at some time during the voyage which position to aim for. The main problem with the radio was that it was dependent on weather conditions and some days we could not get through at all.

The day tended to revolve around the radio. Breakfast was before the first schedule, though as we moved west we started to have breakfast later. Lunch we would have before the afternoon schedule. For breakfast in the first few weeks we had eggs, beans and coffee, and would sit together talking about the kind of night we'd had, and any problems or any experiences we wanted to share. People often think that being alone on a small boat for days on end we'd become bored with each other, but in fact we did not get to spend enough time together for that. One person is on watch as the other one sleeps. There were times of the day when we would take the time to be relaxed together. We enjoyed breakfast and the hour in the evening before sunset. Time spent at sea is so special, you don't need to talk often; there is a communication that happens anyway. Maybe because there are no distractions and our senses were so alive we felt we could communicate without words.

The first month was beautiful. There was little wind but just enough to keep us moving, sometimes with the motor and sometimes sailing. We were not heading north but north-west, so managed to keep sailing on the starboard tack. We were about 1,000 miles offshore, way beyond the gale warnings we heard for Tehuantepec, the infamous stormy Gulf cutting into the southern area of Mexico; but we were meanwhile in a gentle breeze. The Pacific Ocean is extraordinarily alive, and every day we saw some sea life. Dolphins were with us constantly and we never tired of them. We saw turtles, and I remembered hearing stories of sailors who would catch them for food. They are so beautiful it seemed unjustifiable unless it was a matter of survival. Sometimes we saw sharks, eerily gliding through the water. The birds gave us the most amusement: booby birds that would fly 30-40 feet above the water all day and then land on the boat at night to rest. Their contact with humans has been non-existent, so they have no fear. A few times, they would position themselves over the hatch and I would be scared they would peck me. One day a large booby bird about 30 inches tall, of dark brown coloration with a white belly, its large beak greenish and its feet yellow, made itself at home in the cockpit. It was pecking at the lines, so Charles tried to shoo it away. It looked at him, its head cocked to one side, not understanding. Charles finally took a towel and pushed it overboard. It landed in the water, looked puzzled, shook itself off then flew back onto the boat. This happened three times before it finally took the hint and flew up to the spreaders. These extraordinary birds live their lives out at sea, going into land only to have their young. Their hunting tactics are spectacular, often involving straight-as-a-plummet dives from a height of about a hundred feet into the sea, where they swallow the fish they've targeted before resurfacing. The sea was not too rough, so Charles went in the sea most days for his shower. I am not too fond of the water, and nothing would induce me to get in the ocean with that feeling of bottomless fathoms below and images of sharks silently creeping by. Just watching Charles would send a cold shiver up my spine. I would make do with a bucket on the foredeck. We had no water tanks so used the bucket to fetch water for washing and some cooking. We had to get our fresh water from containers on deck also, but we were so used to doing it by the time we left that it didn't seem like work.

We both enjoyed reading and had a lot of books on board, including other sailing adventures such as *Far Tortuga* and *Moby Dick*. In the evening, we liked to listen to the BBC. We heard the news, plays and music. Best of all, however, was the ocean: the sunset every evening, the sunrise every morning, different every time we saw it. There was always a fair amount of work to do, though it was less in the first few weeks when the weather was so mild. Toward the end of March, as we passed the Revillagigedo Islands, a Mexican group of islands lying 600 kilometers off the country's western coast, we had to head more northerly, and the currents seemed stronger.

The engine had been used frequently and was still giving us constant problems. The exhaust was falling apart, and we were repairing it with tin cans and duct tape. Every couple of days it would have rusted through in a new spot and so we would cover the spot with another can, an assortment of glues, duct tape and hose clamps. She was burning a lot of oil, but we had brought a lot with us. The engine was at least going, however, keeping us heading north in those times of no wind.

Our fresh vegetables lasted a month: cabbages, potatoes, onions and pumpkins lasting particularly well. Our salted fish made sumptuous meals. After soaking them in fresh water and cooking them, they tasted as fresh as fish bought in a supermarket. We had cheese, Edam and Gouda, wrapped in wax; and eggs covered in Vaseline and turned over every two weeks to prevent the yolks from sticking to the shell. It wasn't until the second month that I started to get into the tin supply.

Sundays we always tried to make a festive day. Maybe I would make a cake or have a cocktail or open a tin of smoked oysters. We tried to avoid all but the necessary chores. Things rarely broke on Sundays. The engine tended to cooperate, although we tried not to use it. We didn't mind not making much progress as long as we did not go backwards. I was fascinated by the Ham radio and listened to the various nets, trying to pick up the language in case I needed to use it myself. It wasn't until we started heading north that we met any adverse weather. Sleeping on our bed of marijuana we tended to sleep extremely heavily, much more so than I had ever slept at sea before. Normally we would wake up for a change of watch or wind shift, but on this trip we always had a hard time waking out of our deep stoned sleep.

Toward the end of March, slightly north of the Revillagigedo Islands, when Charles was on watch, I was wakened simultaneously by Charles screaming at me and what sounded like a bomb. The bowsprit had snapped off, so the mast was in danger of crashing to the deck. I got up quickly to help avert total disaster. We brought the flaying sails under control and made sure the mast was secured, then decided to have a cup of coffee before carrying on. On examining the bowsprit, we found the wood was rotting inside. It had clearly rotted at some point previously and been fixed with epoxy, but badly fixed. I was furious with the owner for assuring me that it was in perfect condition, and even more with myself for having taken his word and not checked it out. Well, what could we do now? We needed a bowsprit. The part that had broken off was about four feet long. It was still attached to the whisker stays, bobstay and forestay. We disconnected it from the forestay and tried to work out what to do next. Clearing out what was left in the sleeve and then putting the four foot we had left through the sleeve seemed to be the most sensible course of action. It would give us a bowsprit, even if just a short one.

It took the next six days to achieve this. Motoring along with the mizzen up, the wind continued to howl causing mountainous seas. Charles was hanging off the bow attached with his safety harness, chiseling the old bowsprit out of the sleeve. He was almost constantly under water. All I could do was keep him supplied with hot drinks. I offered to do my share and wasn't overly disappointed when he pointed out there was no sense in both of us getting wet. After five days of constant work, we had cleared the sleeve. Then we had to shorten the whisker stays and bobstay and finally we were ready to attach the forestay and raise the sails. We tried to pull up the mainsail, but it wouldn't move; the halyard had come out of its sleeve at the top of the mast. We pulled up the foresail. Of course, the shortened bowsprit changed the angle and both our headsails were too large. The day after a lot of hard work, all was again secured. Charles finished his stint under the water and the wind and seas disappeared. How the new bowsprit was to work we were about to see.

CHAPTER FIVE

STRANDED AT SEA

While Charles had worked at fixing the bowsprit, I had tried to communicate our problems with Jim to let him know that our ability to get to San Francisco was seriously impaired, and maybe we should make the rendezvous at Brenda off San Diego. We were probably 500 miles south-west of San Diego, and I had managed to communicate with one of Jim's associates. At that point, we were 100 miles south of 30' north, but I gave him a message using the code for 25' north. The next time we made contact was after we had fixed everything and he told us a rendezvous had been arranged 100 miles west of our present position and at 25' north. I tried to tell him that this was unreasonable as we were much closer to the United States than he was allowing for, but he said he was simply relaying messages. So after fighting for the last week to get north, we then had to turn around and head south-west.

Oh, how beautiful it was! The wind had dropped, the seas had calmed, and we flew downwind. Was it the same ocean? We watched those hard-fought-for miles disappear. Our rendezvous day was 14 April, and we made the 300 miles in fine time; and then began the waiting. The excitement at 6 p.m. on the 14th was high. The idea of suddenly seeing another boat arrive, all the plans and dreams came flooding back. We had fantasized the entire trip about what to do with our money. Both of us wanted to buy a boat. Charles had seen a boat in Panama, a small catamaran he had liked, and I already had a deposit on a 30-foot wooden boat in Bequia, a Colin Archer. We went through the boating magazines on board looking at equipment for our new boats. Then 7 p.m. came and went but still no boat appeared in sight. We were slightly disappointed, but we could wait. We had other magazines that mentioned restaurants; these were to be our main reading material for the next weeks.

We scanned the horizon constantly, backwards and forwards, making sure we were always spot on our position at 6 p.m. During the planning with Jim in Panama City we had chosen common names for the boats. They were to be *Wind song* and we were to be *Sundancer*. We tried to call them at other times as well as at 6 p.m., when we kept our Ham schedule. We were unsuccessful in contacting anyone. On one of the nets, we heard some phenomena being discussed which were interfering with communications. At least it was not our radio. By the 19th, we were becoming despondent. Was our navigation as good as we thought? The Loran was giving contradictory signals, so we were not bothering with it. On the night of the 19th the moon was full, and the sea shone in its light all around us; its ghostly hue seemed to underline the emptiness. Slowly across the horizon we saw lights and the outline of a ship. We called them up on the VHF; they were en route to Los Angeles. They confirmed our position, which was welcome at that point, and offered to contact anyone in the USA to give them any news of us when they arrived there. We declined their kind offer, but we chatted for a while and then they went on their way.

Could there have been any mistake over the position of our rendezvous point? It would help if we could contact Jim. The 20th dawned, another glorious day. The wind was blowing about 15 knots, but we were keeping our position with the use of the mizzen and the number one jib. Nothing. The 21st was one of those days that for many years had been a special day to me; in my early sailing days I had made a couple of important decisions on 21 April, and as sailors tend to be a superstitious group the day had taken on magical significance in my mind. I told Charles that we would find them that day. At 4 p.m. that afternoon, as I made a cup of tea, I picked up the VHF and idly tried for the umpteenth time: "*Wind song*, *Wind song*, this is *Sundancer*. Do you read me?" I put it down hardly expecting a reply, but about two minutes later we heard "Yea! Is that you, *Wind song*? ... or am I *Wind song*?" then "Hey Bridget, is that you?"

I was delighted and horrified at the same time. Horrified at how unprofessional they were, talking like that on channel 16, using my name which there was no reason for them to know. The main emotion, though, was sheer excitement. We had waited for this moment for two months: the handing over of our cargo for the next stage of the trip had nearly arrived. We had already started rationing our food and were being particularly careful with our water consumption, so we were overjoyed to think we would be able to head for port. "Hello *Wind song*, this is *Sundancer*. Switch to channel 68."

We switched channels, and I continued: "Hey, we sure are happy to hear you guys. We were beginning to think that no one would show up. Where are you?"

"Hey, same here; we are almost out of supplies and we're ready to go home, man. Been out here too long!" How long did they think that we had been out there? "Anyway, we'll be there in about an hour. Just hang on."

I assumed that they must have a radio direction-finding unit on their VHF as they sounded so definite. Charles and I hugged each other. I was so excited that I wanted to start pulling bales out on deck. Charles talked me out of that, but I did start moving the bales about. We celebrated with a pot of coffee and opened three cans. One hour passed, back on the radio.

"How are you guys doing?"

"Great, we'll be there soon. Look out, as we have a strobe light." So we were not upset to see the large red sun sink into the ocean, thinking that it would be much easier to see the strobe light. Then 7 p.m. came.

"How are you doing?" I asked.

"Well we're not really sure. Our Loran isn't too accurate. It gives a reading and then changes. Can you find us?"

"Well where are you? I'm not sure if our direction-finder is giving decent signals; we can't talk and check signals at the same time, so can you keep on and we'll try."

"Hey man, we just want to get this over with. Where are you?"

I gave them our position and told them there were some great stars and planets to take sights from.

They answered, "We don't know how to do that and we have no sextant on board." We talked on and off. They were not keen on talking; they said they wanted some rest. I wanted to check in every hour, but they didn't. They said they would call me. This last exchange came around midnight. I waited for them to call; nothing. At 4 a.m. I tried them; nothing. We tried and tried; nothing all day, and it was a gray, gray day. We called and called, not leaving the radio. We were so depressed that we couldn't even talk to each other. We did not want to verbalize our disappointment.

The next day we got in touch with Jim again. He had assumed we had offloaded, and all was well. He was upset to hear our news and told us to hang on where we were for a time and he would be back in touch. We told him about our water situation, and he asked if we needed it immediately. We said that we could hang on for a week, feeling better for his concern. We wondered if he intended to fly out and drop us water. We felt better and settled into night watches in a happier frame of mind than the previous day. It was three days before we heard from Jim again. He wanted to know if we could get to position Brenda. We said yes, doing something again would be enjoyable. Also, if we were closer to land the Loran might work so we wouldn't have the same problem. We let Jim know that we wanted someone who could navigate. Again he said that he would be in touch and that we should stay put.

The following day I went to tune into the BBC. What was happening? The BBC couldn't be located, and the radio sounded peculiar. Worried, I turned to our local frequency, and there were no Ham conversations. Something was seriously wrong with the radio. We missed our morning schedule, and I became obsessed with trying to fix it before the next one. It seemed that all of the bands had shifted. I finally located the Ham bands. Now I had the problem of equating them with their frequencies, so I could work out where Jim might be. Luckily I had been listening to the nets for the last two months so knew I should be able to identify them and then move up the required number to locate our frequency. I didn't have it perfected but worked on it all day. I found what I thought was the frequency but could not contact Jim. I tried to summon the courage to talk on the net; maybe the problem was a common one and someone would tell me what to do. It was certainly worth a try. I was heard but distorted. No one understood what I was saying though they were trying, and no one recognized what was wrong with the radio. The frequencies were constantly moving, and I could follow them to hear, but when I had to talk my voice became distorted. On the third day, I managed to find Jim. I could follow him by moving the dial carefully. Now the difficult thing to do was to let him know our present problem and work out how to communicate. The next morning we managed. Jim would ask me yes and no questions and I would key the mike. In this way we set up our next meeting, 300 miles off San Diego in five days' time. A boat was supposedly coming from San Diego that could navigate, had a Ham radio and a VHF.

STRANDED AT SEA

We headed north-east, sailing hard to make our new rendezvous point. We were happy again, full of energy and back to our dreams. I wanted to bring my kid brother back to the Caribbean to help me fix up my new boat. He felt very lost back home. I had sailed with him when he was eight years old, and he was a born sailor. I imagined family and friends' faces as I turned up with that special gift or flew in to see them. We had about 20 knots of wind the whole trip, so made good speed. The waves and currents were knocking us south, but we were still making enough distance north to make our new rendezvous point. We were sailing with just the mizzen and headsail which didn't fit right due to the shortened bowsprit. The main halyard was out of its track so we could not pull the main up. If it had been totally necessary Charles would have gone up to fix it; he had done it before when we had left Taboga. Only the main halyard went as far as the top of the mast as she was a three-quarter rig, meaning that when we pulled Charles up on the foresail he then had to climb out of his bosun's chair and stand on it and climb the mast. We were not going to do this in a rough sea in our weakened condition unless it was absolutely vital, as had been the case when he went up to fix the spreaders rolling dangerously from side to side.

Our supplies had been sufficient for two months, but were becoming sparse. We had plenty of dried beans, dried soups but no water. We had been having a pint a day each for three weeks, and this we reduced to half a pint a day between us, deciding our final two gallons could possibly last thirty days. I rationed the food, hoping to make it last the same amount of time. If things worked out before then, we still had what was necessary to make port. We had plenty of vitamins as we hadn't bothered using them on the earlier part of the trip, our diet being adequate. We dug out some old cans of food that had been left in the galley sometime before I took over the boat: a case of army supply apple sauce and a packet of prunes. Maybe they even pre-dated the owner. Breakfast became two vitamins pills, a prune and a sip of water each. For lunch, I took half a packet of soup or sauce and mixed it with steak sauce and fried it as four tiny pancakes. We ate these nibbling slowly, commenting on which made the better pancake. The apple sauce we had nearly finished before we reached our next rendezvous position. We would mix it with powdered milk and thought it was delicious. We planned on making it for friends ashore. How relative things are. The thought of it now makes me feel ill, but at the time it was elixir. Any food supplies we had that could be prepared without fresh water were limited. We still had salted fish, but it was uneatable without fresh water, as were beans and rice. The pasta we cooked in sea water and mixed half a tin of whatever we had left, mainly green vegetables with six strands of spaghetti each. We savored them slowly, making each mouthful last. For the next three weeks, this was our daily diet. Unfortunately we could not just sit around conserving energy as there was a steady 15-20 knots of wind most of the time and a strong current running against us, so to stay in one spot meant sailing hard all day, tacking each change of watch. We just made sure that we were in position at 6 p.m. twice a day for the rendezvous.

We had read all the books I had kept accessible and now were moving bales to get at the ones I hadn't bothered to keep out, mainly science fiction which we devoured avidly. One of the last books I read was a story of a couple whose boat sank, and they lived for 117 days in a life raft, eating birds and drinking their blood to survive. The Ham radio we heard and sometimes didn't. Usually it was Jim with another excuse: "Sorry, there have been some problems. They'll be there in a few days."

We talked about how long we could hold out and what our options were. Jim had told me about some other people who had done a trip for him and had run out of food so had dinghied ashore for supplies. We didn't think that he would appreciate us dumping the cargo; after all, we were in no danger, just out of water. We looked at the charts and the pilot. We could go to the Revillagigedo Islands, back downwind; or to Isla Guadalupe, 140 miles off Baja California; or to the mainland. We discussed our options but put off making any decision. Eventually, after three weeks of waiting, we realized that we had to do something.

"OK, let's try Isla Guadalupe."

We agreed.

CHAPTER SIX

THE SCREAM AT ISLA GUADALUPE

The decision was made. We hadn't actually had any choice, under the circumstances: the water had been rationed for six weeks now, and for four weeks we'd had just half a pint a day to share between us. Food supplies had dwindled away; our cupboards were almost bare with mainly dried beans and dried soup packets. Our dreams and our faith were not enough to sustain us. Our two solar stills (to turn salt water into fresh) had failed, and the horizon, empty in all directions, reinforced the necessity for us to go in search of supplies, finally accepting that they were not going to come to us. The cargo of marijuana was worth so much to so many and didn't even belong to us, so we felt we should do everything we could to save it. We had lived 98 days now in a cramped space, working hard for twenty-four hours a day and suffering deprivations we had never even imagined. We needed some reward to make it all worthwhile. No, we weren't ready to give up just yet.

We smiled at each other: any decision, however fraught with danger, was better than the eternal waiting. Easing the sheets, *Saada* started to move east, reaching out to new horizons after three weeks of fighting to stay in one spot. It was 7 a.m. and the start of a beautiful new day. A shimmering orange sun was sending flashes of light through the wavelets as 8-10 knots of wind from the north-east blew us on our way. Feeling exhilarated, I went to fetch our breakfast; and somehow, even our daily two vitamin pills and two prunes seemed more appetizing than usual. Charles's frown had disappeared and together we started to make new plans. That in itself was a joy, as the twice daily disappointment of the rendezvous boat's non-appearance had taken its toll. Now all was positive again. We were back in charge and no longer dependent on others. Unfortunately we had no chart of our destination, but that seemed a trifle and not worth worrying about. The pilot that we'd read and discussed at times in the past few weeks was now brought out and studied in detail:

Isla de Guadalupe (29 02'N, 118 17'W) lying about 140 miles off the coast of Baja California, is about 20 miles long and nearly 7 miles wide... The island consists of a chain of high, volcanic mountain ridges which rise to an elevation of 4257 ft near its N end. The shores are bold and rugged and may be safely approached within half a mile. The South part of the island is barren but there are fertile valleys and trees in the North part. The peaks are obscured by clouds over the greater part of the year but when visible can be seen at distances of up to 60 miles. Anchorage can be taken close inshore in a small cove on the east side of the island about one and a half miles S of Punta del Norte, the N point of the island... South of the point of rocks at the S end of the above anchorage there is a small sandy beach where good anchorage can be taken about quarter of a mile offshore.

Isla Guadalupe's closeness to the United States border was unquestionably a worry, as it was such an obvious place for smuggling adventures. Would it be patrolled? Whatever the risks, our options had run out. To run back downwind to the Revillagigedo Islands would take too long and the pilot described them as barren, thus less chance of finding water. Even if we could not find water on Isla Guadalupe, we could hide our cargo somewhere and sail to the mainland to re-supply and contact our boss.

Charles, though, felt uneasy as he had encountered problems with the Mexican Guardia years before in Acapulco, but could not think of an alternative. They had stopped him for no reason and would not let him go till he had paid them quite a lot of money. They did not have a good reputation, and he didn't want to repeat the experience. Despite that, he was happy to feel in charge of his own destiny again. However, we discussed at considerable length the possibility of running into the Mexican Guardia: "We'll scuttle the boat as soon as we see them," we concluded seriously. This was a simple statement, but we meant it. We had both heard smuggling stories of scuttling boats: "There we were, the Coast Guard about to board. I gave the signal. Bill opened up the sea cocks and down she went." In preparation for this terrible event happening, we packed a suitcase to take on the life raft with us: clothes, navigation instruments, photos, books and emergency equipment.

It continued to be a perfect day. Up above, the sun glowed in a clear blue sky and the gentle breeze remained steady enough to push us along at 4 knots, speeding after the endless fight against wind and current as we had travelled north. We pictured the island in our minds, dependent on the pilot's description. Would there be a decent beach to land the dinghy on? We remembered other times of overturning dinghies as we brought them into beaches. Offloading close to 200 bales of marijuana would entail a lot of heavy manual work. How far would we have to carry them? We would have to ensure they were well hidden as well as protected from weather and wildlife. Images from a medley of different books came to mind, little Cornish coves, hidden caves, protective bushes and more.

The sun started to disappear into the sea, casting a red glow over the western sky. We settled happily into our night watch after eating our ration of spaghetti with more relish than before. The breeze remained steady enough to keep sailing, and we had exciting new fantasies to while away the night hours. We had to remain alert with new concerns. The fear of a boat engine or a light on the horizon was ever-present. The realization that we were moving further and further into Mexican waters and the 200-mile fishing limit made running into a patrol boat a distinct possibility. We kept the VHF on continuously, though as it had been silent for so long, it was easy to forget. Suddenly at 3 a.m. we heard, "This is US Coast Guard Long Beach reading you." The crisp American voice exploded into the quiet night. "Charles, it's the US Coast Guard!" Tiredness, strain, lack of food and water are not conducive to sensible thinking, so it took a few minutes to realize that though 200 miles offshore, we were picking up US Coast Guard at Long Beach. Of course, we could only hear their side of the conversation, and that gave the impression they were talking to us. How strange it sounded after 99 days at sea. It brought home to us the reality of our situation, the unfortunate illegality of our enterprise.

Then 24 May dawned. This was the day we hoped to arrive. Our fantasies saw us arriving late in the afternoon, anchoring in a calm, deserted bay, going ashore to find our cave and water, spending the night taking off the cargo, bringing on water and setting off for San Diego the following morning. It never occurred to me that it wouldn't work out just like this. As we got closer to land, our Loran finally began to make sense. It was a pleasant confirmation of our celestial sights. There are times when, marking positions on a chart, you begin to wonder about your position; this is not due to lack of confidence in the ability to take good sights. After prolonged periods at sea, you enter another world and it becomes hard to relate to the significance of the chart. So the day progressed, the hours marched by, the miles slipped away, and the breeze disappeared. Oh well, we wouldn't know what to do with ourselves if nothing went wrong! Charles had enjoyed a welcome day off from the engine, but now he descended into the engine room once again to bleed the fuel system and start her up.

We saw the island from 15 miles away at 11 a.m. It was strange to see land after three months; when the horizon, unbroken except for fantasy islands created by clouds, starts to take a firmer outline, and you know it's land. Normally you can smell the land before you see it, but for some reason, this was not the case with Isla Guadalupe.

As usual the engine was not cooperating, but today's problem was a new one: it was severe overheating. Water had stopped coming out of the exhaust, and upon investigation we realized the problem was chronic rust throughout the system. No sooner would we clear out one part than another part would seize up. This slowed our progress, and we worried whether we'd have enough daylight to explore the island on arrival, still believing we'd be safely anchored by nightfall.

Isla Guadalupe was the strangest looking island I'd ever seen, though how much that impression was created by our state of minds at the time I don't know. It appeared extremely forbidding, almost primitive and most unwelcoming. As we moved along the north coast around 5 p.m., nursing the engine, it seemed we traveled into another era. All was still, not a ripple on the water, and on the prehistoric-looking island there was no sign of life, not only human life, but there were no birds and no trees. It seemed that nothing could live there except maybe some forgotten monster from another age. I was to learn many years later that the waters around Isla Guadalupe boast the best collection of great white sharks in the Western Hemisphere and are known by divers worldwide as the "Great White Heaven."

Anticipating the hard work ahead, we opened the last can of soda which I'd hidden, and mixed it with the juice from a tin of blueberries. No glass of champagne could have tasted so delicious. It was getting dark as we turned south at the north-east corner of the island and headed down the coast searching for the bay mentioned in the pilot. It was an eerie night, silent except for the noise of the engine. Night descended fast, and it was a black night with no moon, only the dark outline of the island so close; no light to help us see the coast, the bay or the beach. I brought out the searchlight, so proudly bought in Panama three months earlier, but it was useless. It was, in fact, the headlight from a car and lit the water right next to the boat but showed us no details on the land. Actually, it disturbed our night vision, so we put it away.

I was beginning to feel tired. In the six or seven months this adventure had been going on, I'd managed to keep total faith in it all working out, but all of a sudden I felt tired. Being close to an unknown coast at night is always frightening, yet here we were, no chart, no moon, just frightfully close to land. Where were the rocks mentioned? Were we inside the bay? There seemed to be land on three sides now. Charles had gone forward with the anchor. Communicating with each other was hard because the engine was so noisy and we had to keep all the engine room hatches open to help with the overheating. Suddenly in the darkness we saw a light flash.

It was there for less than a minute, but it was there. Charles had seen it too. What was it? A house? Another boat? We looked and waited, but again, all we saw was black and black, and we could hear the waves splash on the rocks, so, so close. The tiredness I was experiencing was dangerously close to becoming despair. I mustn't let Charles see. (Many months later, I discovered that he had been feeling the same, but was hiding it from me.) We decided all we could do was anchor and wait until morning, so Charles went back to the bow. I stayed at the tiller steering, it seemed, straight into a cliff. I needed to urinate, but was wearing so many layers of clothes as well as full foul-weather gear that I didn't manage to get them off in time. I felt tears starting to run down my face as I realized I was wetting myself. No, no, I must be strong, I mustn't give into despair. Charles had dropped the anchor, and it hadn't even touched the bottom. He came aft to discuss what we should do next. He was smiling and full of positive energy, which made me feel better. Of course, we should have realized that as the island was volcanic, it would be too deep to anchor, but our brains had known better days. The windless still, still sea seemed to be the only thing going for us. We weren't moving, so we decided to stay where we were and take it in turns to get some sleep. Even our bed was in chaos because, assuming we wouldn't be sleeping on top of our bed of marijuana again, I'd been packing and reorganizing. I slept first, just crawling into a small space, my head on a suitcase, still in my foul-weather gear and my wet clothes underneath.

When Charles woke me three hours later, I got up more reluctantly than any time previously. He looked so tired and quickly crawled into the space I'd vacated, as I sat out in the black night having the longest three hours I'd ever lived through. The sea remained as eerily still as earlier, and the land looked close enough to touch, reaching up to the sky. All around came the strangest most frightening sounds I'd ever heard, the shrieks of some kind of wild animals. I sat, suddenly determined that whatever else happened, we would not set foot on that island. It's strange to realize, even as we get older, how comforting the daylight can be and how, as the darkness goes, so do many of the nightmares; not all the nightmares disappeared, however, as the sounds we'd heard had not been imaginary.

In the morning a small settlement became visible, small wooden shacks standing in a small valley, now seen between the gray forbidding cliffs. Not a green fertile valley, more like a fissure caused by some monumental movement of the earth some centuries before. What was this place? Who were these people? Shivering, I watched Charles row ashore. I saw men come down to meet him. There seemed to be no women or children, just men. I looked around the island, as forbidding a place as it had seemed the previous day. On the beaches, there seemed to be hundreds of dead seals. Oh no, that must have been the awful noises we'd heard during the night, we must have stumbled into a seal-slaughtering community. I looked back toward Charles just in time to see him disappearing down a pit, a group of men surrounding him. Panic started to descend on me. What should I do? Another group of men were readying one of the dinghies and pointing toward me. I had a sudden vision of the cannibals on Robinson Crusoe's Island. I made a pathetic kind of attempt to shield the marijuana with a sail I needed to sew. It didn't hide anything, but I needed to do something. My tiredness and lack of food and water seemed to have dulled my brain to a point where there was nothing I could do. I stared at the group on the beach, who seemed to have changed their mind about coming out to me. I looked back at Charles. How dramatically the world can change. The sun was shining, Charles was out of his pit, and coming back down toward the beach, carrying our water jugs. As I looked back toward the beach, all the seals were waking up. I started to laugh and smile. With a new zest for our adventure, I finally took off my filthy clothes and changed. I put on the kettle for a pot of coffee, ready for Charles, who arrived full of the joy of life and laden down with food and water. The men ashore had filled a box with tins of chicken, ham, eggs, crackers, cookies. We were ecstatic. If the whole trip had worked out exactly as planned, we couldn't have been happier than we were at that moment. It was a moment of pure joy, preceded by despair and followed by disaster.

We decided to stay and have breakfast before leaving. As we happily sat there, I saw Charles's face suddenly tighten before he reached out and grabbed the binoculars. "A gunboat," he gasped. In retrospect, we might have handled everything differently; but at that time, we were physically exhausted, suffering from dehydration, and the extremes of emotion in the last twelve hours had not helped. Charles wanted to sink the boat where we sat. "No, let's get away." "Let's run for it." "Quick, turn on the engine." "Hey, we forgot the anchor." "Pull up the anchor." "The engine's overheating." "We can't help it; we've got to get out of their way." I looked toward the gunboat, a gray vessel about 200 foot long with menacing-looking guns on her foredeck aiming straight at us. So with the navy coming into the bay, we limped out of it, anchor still down and engine smoking. Turning the engine on and off, we managed to clear the east coast and head north until the engine finally failed us in an interesting array of cracks, splutters and noise.

We sat there: no wind, no engine, just 2,000 pounds of marijuana and a Mexican gunboat five minutes away. So here it was: that moment we had so calmly discussed, the moment to scuttle the boat. Many inanimate objects seem to take on personalities, but none more than a boat. Both Charles and I had both had a long, emotional history with *Saada* and on this trip it had taken her a long time to trust us, but after she had we knew she would protect us. She had. She had been our home, our protector, and our companion for five months, and now we had to drown her. Again with hindsight, we understood why it had been so hard not only emotionally but also physically to achieve. She was a steel boat with large fuel and water tanks built into her hull. These were all empty now, full of air, so simply cutting the inlet hoses was not enough. She started to fill with water, but not enough to sink her.

The morning hours of 25 May 1981 were a living nightmare. We moved as if in a bad movie, one moment sinking the boat and the next moment we saw a gray whale, so close to the boat we could almost touch her. That must be a sign we weren't meant to sink the boat, so we started bailing her out, all the while eating our way through a box of marshmallows the islanders had given us, drinking our prized bottle of Dom Pérignon champagne that we had hidden for the end of our trip, and crying and smoking our way through 200 cigarettes. We had both successfully given up cigarettes, but the islanders had put a carton in with the box of food. Bailing her out wasn't much more successful than filling her up had been. Maybe we should sink the marijuana. We tied a bale to our large Honda generator, but the bale kept it afloat. At this point, we heard over the VHF the Guardia calling another gunboat and talking about us.

It was hard to follow all they said, but we understood enough to panic even more and so we returned to the plan of sinking our beautiful boat. We brought out our bilge pumps and started filling the empty tanks with water; meanwhile, we got our suitcase and provisions into the dinghy. The deal was for me to take off just before she went down, then Charles would launch the life raft at the last minute, and we would get into it with all our things. At this point, we saw the naval vessel leaving the bay. Poor *Saada*, despite her valiant efforts, was beginning to take water through her ports. It seemed only a matter of minutes before she would sink. The naval vessel turned west at the north-east point of the island. Was it going to ignore us? I had climbed into the dinghy and was watching *Saada*, who began first to bury her bow and then fight back again. I looked round at the naval vessel. She was turning toward us. At that point, as I sat, from the depth of my being came a scream: the realization never even remotely considered before that we were going to fail, going to be arrested, locked up in a Mexican dungeon for decades. The scream, which seemed separate from me, rose up and disappeared into the air; with this outburst I suddenly adapted to the new situation, watching tensely as every second *Saada* seemed about to disappear forever. Charles threw the life raft, which opened in a rush of color, fluorescent orange and purple with a flashing light at the top of the little circus tent. I rowed to meet him and climbed aboard, and together we sat, holding hands, watching as the naval vessel approached us. They changed their mind and turned to *Saada*, still fighting for her life while I clutched valiantly at Charles's hand, thinking only that now I'd never be a mother. This thought came out of nowhere but hit me with extraordinary force and pain. We watched the Mexican Navy secure *Saada* before sending an inflatable raft to pick us up. As we climbed on board, stunned and empty of emotion, I looked at our floating tent and tiredly remarked to Charles, "I'm not sure I could have survived 117 days in that."

CHAPTER SEVEN

A MEXICAN GUN BOAT

The inflatable dinghy headed across the calm sea toward the naval vessel with Charles and me and three Mexican sailors on board. The sailors were polite, friendly and showed much concern for us. They were towing our life raft with our possessions in it. We drew along the starboard side of the gunboat, *Saada* was tied to the port side, and lifelessly we crawled up the ladder. Greeted on the deck by more caring officers, we were at every moment waiting for the handcuffs, waiting to be led away, locked up and separated. When would we see each other again?

We were led down a flight of stairs into a paneled room with a large wooden table in the center, big enough to seat eight to ten. Off to the right as we entered was a comfortable sitting room with a television set playing something or other. The corridor continued on past the dining room. We sat down and were offered coffee which we drank gratefully. There was noise in the background: sailors rushing backwards and forwards, engines, pumps, so much activity, so many people, so difficult to take it all in. We devoured one cup of coffee after another. The sailor who was pouring our coffee kept filling our cups. An officer was seated at the end of the table, a tall, dark man with a moustache. He smiled at us and asked us how we were. Did they know? Charles and I looked at each other. When was the interrogation going to start? Were they playing with us?

"Where have you come from?" The question was asked not so

much as an interrogation, more like one sailor chatting to another.

"Panama. Oh, I never visit Panama."

His English was broken, but he was trying to make conversation. Charles responded to him in Spanish and together they chatted about Panama and Mexico, the difference in accents and other conversational topics. I sat there not sure what was happening, waiting for the feeling of unreality that had descended on me to pass. I sat drinking more and more coffee. A sailor passed through and winked at us. "*Buena mota*," he murmured, Mexican slang for marijuana. Well, they had found it. It would have been difficult not to, but it was the first indication that anyone had seen it.

Eventually the Captain appeared, a dark man of about thirty-two, medium height, clean-shaven with a pleasant face. The look in his eyes was confusing. We were ready for the confrontation, the harsh, accusatory face of our captor, and instead he looked at us with compassion and guilt as if he was asking our forgiveness. He came in with papers, shook our hands and sat down. He asked us if we spoke Spanish as his English was not too fluent. He explained that he was not a policeman but a naval captain, so he was not arresting us but, because of the nature of our cargo, he was duty bound to take us to Ensenada and hand us over to the proper authorities. He had some questions he wanted to ask us, but he wanted to give us time to change, wash and rest first. He told us that they were going to leave *Saada* at the island for another gunboat to tow to Ensenada. With that said, he instructed someone to conduct us to his cabin, show us the shower and bring us our suitcase. We could feel the boat begin to move. We could see nothing but could imagine poor *Saada* watching us leave.

We stood together in the captain's cabin, actually a small cabin, but it seemed enormous after our cramped quarters. There was a mirror on one wall, a single bed against the other. I looked at myself, the first mirror I had seen since leaving Panama. Was that me? My face was gaunt, the bones pronounced. Slowly I took off all my clothes and looked at my emaciated body. I had always had fantasies, growing up in the 1960s, of looking like Twiggy or Jean Shrimpton. I had never been fat but never skinny either. Now for the first time I saw how I looked with no spare fat – terrible. I was staring at a figure straight out of an Oxfam poster. My breasts, never large, were now not only non-existent, but I had an indentation where they had once been. At least my spirit had not been equally devastated as I managed a smile when remembering the agony I had suffered in my late teens trying to achieve this amount of weight loss, and now I had finally managed, and this was what I looked like.

The shower was in a room the other side of the corridor. We gathered our things and went to it. Charles turned on the water. It gushed out, all that water, how beautiful it looked. I went to step in and stopped: "It's ice, it will kill me if I step under that." Charles could not wait and did not care how cold it was. He leapt under the freezing, rushing water and with a look of exhilaration washed himself all over, including his hair with the Captain's shampoo. He managed to turn on the warm water before I gingerly stepped under the warm cleansing flow.

Back in the Captain's cabin we dressed in clean clothes. After the weeks at sea, it felt strange to be clean without salt clinging to our skin. My skirt, which had always been tight, now hung over my hips looking six sizes too large. We sat on the bed and looked at each other. If this had been a movie, we would fall into one another's arms and make passionate love, knowing we were about to be separated for years. Unfortunately this wasn't a movie, and we just felt drained and sad, so sat holding hands a short time without saying anything. For six months now we had been together day and night and had grown tremendously close, so we both felt the inevitable, impending separation with an immense sorrow that needed no words. We didn't feel like resting, so went back out to face we knew not quite what.

Back in the dining room was yet another officer: tall and thin, also with a moustache. He rose and shook hands with us, looking us over with interest. He spoke decent English and introduced himself as the doctor. He asked us a few questions about our physical states. He discussed dehydration and told us that it would be a long time before we would be able to eat normally again as our stomachs had shrunk with the rest of us. I found this hard to believe. I felt I could eat an enormous banquet.

There was no suggestion that we were criminals: we were being treated as if we had been picked up after our boat started sinking, and the fact of the illegal cargo was not mentioned. We began to relax and proceeded to drink coffee and water; a sailor was assigned to us to keep us supplied with liquids. We were left alone for a short while, and for the first time verbalized our fears of separation. "Maybe if we got married we could at least write to each other." "Good idea. The captain should be able to marry us, let's ask him." This we did when he next appeared, and he was genuinely sorry that he could not marry us as we were not Mexican citizens and would first need to get permission from the British Embassy.

Over the next fourteen hours we had many conversations with Captain Roberto Gomez and grew to respect him immensely and to feel sorry for the situation he was in. He was young for a captain but obviously exceptionally good at his job. We never heard him shout orders, yet the ship ran perfectly smoothly. He seemed well liked and respected by both his crew and officers. We discussed various subjects. He was a singularly honorable man, and we had presented him with a conflict he had not faced before. Before meeting us, I think he'd had little contact with "criminals" but here we were, the same age as him, similar interests and outlooks. We respected each other, yet he had to turn us over to be imprisoned. While certainly proud of being Mexican, he was ashamed to say that there were, unfortunately, some corrupt members in the Mexican Federal Police. He shared with us as much information as he had on the Mexican legal system and jails, but in reality he knew very little, never having been so closely involved before.

Although Captain Roberto Gomez was the man responsible for our imprisonment, we remember him as the man who helped us feel human again, who gave us the time and strength to deal with what had to follow. For it was a strange interlude, our fourteen hours aboard the naval vessel *Ignacio Vallarta*. They had a video cassette machine and brought out their two English movies for us. We watched *Shogun* that night, and the following morning *Dog Day Afternoon*, a story of a mismanaged bank robbery where one of the robbers was prepared to die rather than go back to jail. Although it was difficult to comprehend that we were on our way to jail, this film simply reinforced our fear.

For dinner, the chef asked me what I would like to eat and eagerly I told him everything. Excited I sat down to salad, chicken, steak, fresh baked bread, potatoes and vegetables; but after two mouthfuls, I was full. The doctor had warned me, but I hadn't believed him. He sat next to me at dinner, watching me with amusement, and told me not to worry. Despite not being able to eat, dinner was enjoyable. The officers were excellent company and seemed to enjoy us as much we enjoyed them. For a time, we forgot what lay ahead. We settled into life aboard the gunboat.

We went to bed early. A sailor was assigned to watch us, though he remained at a respectful distance from us. We slept in bunks in the crew's quarters, and though seriously tired it was hard to sleep. Our bodies were now adapted to our three hours on, three hours off routine; in addition, our minds were ticking over with questions, impressions and worries. Despite the restless night, we felt better in the morning. It was strange not to see the sun come up, not to feel the wind direction nor to see the state of the sea. There is so much to look at in a small boat at sea, the colors always changing. Here we were with man-made colors, grays and browns that did not change with the time of day. I experienced a sudden flash of realization that it would be man-made colors we would be seeing from now on and that our freedom was gone. Sadness laid heavily on me, but nothing showed on the surface. We went back to the officers' quarters to wait out the time till we arrived in Ensenada. Captain Roberto was concerned to help us as much as possible. He promised to contact our Embassy. We also handed over all our possessions to him, specifically passports and money, in various Mediterranean and Caribbean denominations that I had collected over the years. He put them into an envelope and gave us a receipt, a copy of which he kept, and another copy he gave to the Federal Police when they came to take us.

We heard the engines slow down and looked out through the portholes. Ensenada. I could see tuna boats and small fishing boats. How different from the last time I sailed into Ensenada, almost exactly two years earlier. I had been delivering a yacht from San Francisco to the Caribbean with some good friends, and it was my first visit to Central America. I remembered the excitement of entering Mexico for the first time and spending a memorable evening at the legendary Hussong's Cantina, the oldest bar in Mexico! Soon, however, the engines stopped and Charles and I sat there quietly holding hands, trying to give each other comfort and strength, waiting. We heard them coming: brisk stomping feet marching up the gang plank. We were sat in the Captain's sitting room, and I glimpsed two policemen through the door, silver handcuffs held in their hands. A cold fear started creeping through me again. Charles and I clutched one another's hands more tightly. The policemen were shown into the Captain's office as he wished to talk to them.

After about ten minutes, we were called in. The Captain sensed our nervousness and gave us more coffee while the two Federal Police asked us some preliminary questions. The taller one was wearing a gray suit and spectacles. He had a thin mouth, the lips slightly raised at one end in a kind of smirk. He rested his left elbow on the table and glanced at us as we sat down opposite them, no smile or greeting of any kind. His companion was smaller and had greased back, black hair, wore a brown suit and, leaning back in his chair, steely, cold, gray eyes that stared directly at us.

A short while later they stood up and let us know we were leaving. They picked up the handcuffs, looked at us but, surprisingly, didn't put them on us. We followed them up onto the deck where the crew were lined up. As we walked past them, they all wished us luck. And as we passed the officers, each one of them in turn shook our hands and said something to try and give us hope. Not only did this treatment make us feel better, it affected the Federal Officers accompanying us, and they too started to treat us slightly better.

As we left the boat behind us, we walked toward a large white car. The taller man opened the back door and we climbed in. Our two guardians got in the front, and we all drove off. We watched the harbor disappear as we turned into the streets of Ensenada, wondering when, if ever, we might be back by the sea. Maybe not for years, I depressingly realized.

CHAPTER EIGHT

WELCOME TO MEXICO

A short journey brought us to the Federal Police building, at which point we got out and entered. Here, there was a large entrance hall with a desk to the right; straight ahead was a small corridor with two small cells. We were taken through, and both put in one of the cells. It was a square cell about six feet by six feet, with a hard bench against the far wall and a small lavatory in the right corner. We were frisked before being put in the cell, and my handbag was searched. I watched the young policeman go through it. My purse, as always, was filled with a myriad of articles and numerous pieces of paper. My heart dropped when I noticed all the various phone numbers I had and immediately worried that they would now be listed somewhere or even investigated, despite all being totally innocent. I saw the piece of paper I had been given by the sweet old couple on the flight from Miami to San José. Fortunately the young policeman had no interest in phone numbers or addresses. He took the vitamins I had left and then gleefully found half a joint. This made his search a success, so he put everything else back.

We had two neighbors: we couldn't see them, but could hear them, two young men, probably in their early twenties by the sound of it. They sounded cheerful enough, so we passed them some cigarettes; thin fingers stretched out from an unknown body, taking two cigarettes.

"*Gracias, amigos.*"

WELCOME TO MEXICO

There was little to do, cooped up in this cell. We discussed our story: basically the truth, just leaving out any names. If you are caught red-handed with two tons of marijuana, there is little you can say. In a car or a van, with marijuana concealed in door panels, you could always pretend ignorance of its existence; but in the middle of the ocean with the marijuana filling the entire boat, it was difficult to deny. There was nothing to look at except a brick wall. The one window was barred and high up. From the main entrance hall, we could hear sounds of voices from various people and from the television. We had no idea what was happening, or how long we were to remain in this cell; but thankfully we had not been separated.

Eventually an older, kindly looking police officer came and unlocked the cell. He beckoned me; I followed him through the hall and up the stairs. At the top, there was a room with three desks: a large one and two smaller ones. An attractive, smiling woman sat at one of the smaller desks and told me to sit down. The other two desks were occupied by men, one of them being the smaller man who had brought us here. The other was a taller man with spectacles and a balding head. He sat with an air of importance at the larger desk. We were later to discover that this was the District Attorney. The woman was the official interpreter, and she took me through my statement, typing it into Spanish as I spoke. She didn't type very fast, and there were constant interruptions from the two men who interspersed my account with questions. The statement took about one and a half hours to give. I didn't mind, as doing something was better than sitting in the cell waiting and waiting. When I had finished the woman stood up and smiled. She took my hand and squeezed it.

"Don't worry, it won't be too bad. You'll have a good life when you come out."

She scurried off with her papers and left me sitting there. The

SAILING INTO THE ABYSS

D.A. followed her, leaving me with the "fox". He walked backwards and forwards. I could feel his eyes on me as I looked down at my lap. "Let's get to the truth now," he snapped. I glared up at him. I don't know what was in my expression: maybe the weeks of waiting, of suffering, but whatever it was he stepped back. "What do you think?" I said dramatically. "Look at me ... I nearly died out there. Do you think that I would try to protect someone who did this to me?" He looked down rather sheepishly. "OK," he said. He went to the door in time to open it for the D.A. and the interpreter to return. They had bags of chips and barbecued chicken. They gave me a chicken in a bag plus some chips, and a couple of sodas, apologizing that that was all they had. I returned to the cell in triumph with the food. Charles and I sat together and ate as much as we could and gave what we could not eat and a soda to our neighbors, who were not getting the special treatment that we were.

Charles and I had a couple of hours together before he was taken off for his interrogation, and I sat staring at the wall, my mind a blank. I was still unable to deal with our predicament so clung onto each situation, afraid of the next one: this cell was now home, and we were together still. Charles's interrogation was faster than mine, so I wasn't alone for long. Before he returned I was taken upstairs to join him. "What's happening?" I conveyed to him. He shrugged his shoulders unknowingly. The D.A. was suddenly exceptionally friendly. "Come and sit by me," he said. He sat us either side of him, then a man appeared with a camera. We assumed it was for routine mug shots, though it was strange to see how the D.A. preened himself and straightened his hair. The photographer scurried around taking pictures then left. The D.A. apologized, and still we didn't understand why. Another man then appeared, slow and gray-haired. He wanted to ask us some questions. He was a doctor. He tapped us on the back, glanced at our eyes and teeth. Were we horses? He then asked us, through the interpreter, a few questions. His main concern seemed to be our drug habits.

We explained that neither of us had ever taken any drugs other than smoking marijuana or hashish.

"Are you addicts?"

"No."

"How often do you smoke these substances?"

"It depends: at a party or with friends, a few joints; on other days, maybe none."

He wasn't terribly interested. He needed a figure to put on his paper. "One, two or three a day? Every day? How many days a week?" We finally allowed him a joint a day. What that told him I do not know, but it satisfied him, and we were returned to our cell.

The hours ticked by. Our neighbors left: we saw them briefly as they passed by our cell on their way to what ... freedom or jail? At some point, our suitcase was taken into another room. I thought nothing of it, assuming they were checking it. Maybe we would be able to stay together all night. I had to go and add something to my statement. I noticed it was dark outside. On the television an American news channel was giving a weather report. I sat watching it, fascinated, as the interpreter typed out my whole statement again and prepared it for my six signatures. As if to divert my mind from the seriousness of the situation I was in, I began comparing US weather reports with British television weather reports. The US weather man, Captain Mike, had colorful weather maps and colorful quips. On British television the weather man never even changes his expression; soberly dressed, he reports the weather as if delivering a verdict in a trial.

I tried to ascertain from the interpreter if we were spending the night there, and she thought at this point that we probably were. So back in our cell we tried to arrange ourselves to get some rest. All of a sudden the cell was opened and we were off yet again. We climbed into the same white car and set off. We drove through street after street, mainly back streets as we saw no shops and few people. Eventually the car pulled up outside a large gray forbidding-looking building. Bars covered all the windows, or rather slits in the wall. The door was large with a smaller door set into it. My hand tightened inside Charles's larger hand. Was this grim building to be our new home? And if so, for how long?

CHAPTER NINE

HOTEL ENSENADA

The door creaked as it opened. Behind the now open door, all was dark; a large hall, stone floors and various locked steel doors. Holding the door was an old skinny man with a hunched back, furtive eyes and a wizened face. He took the paperwork from our companion who left, wishing us well. We stood there. The old man took Charles to one side, frisked him, unlocked one of the steel doors with a key from a massive key ring with numerous keys upon it that was attached by a chain around his waist and pushed him in. The moment had come. We had been separated. Why couldn't I escape from this feeling of being in a movie? Maybe there was a part of me that just couldn't accept the reality of our situation. Maybe the characters we were meeting seemed like characters we had only seen in movies. I had never before met a wizened old man with a hunchback. One wondered if jobs beget certain characters or vice versa, and also whether he made the jail more sinister or vice versa.

Having locked Charles up, he limped toward me and frisked me, not particularly thoroughly. He took the few dollars I had held on to, wrote how much it was on a scrap of paper which he gave to me, then beckoned me to follow him. We set off down a dank corridor, the keys jangling in his hand, and went through another heavily locked door, down another dank corridor, through yet another locked door, across a small concrete square with clothes hanging up, through another locked door, into a large lit room. He simply pushed me into the room and locked the door. I looked around. The room was spacious, probably 35 by 20 feet. Half of it was raised and along the raised part were a row of mattresses. On the part where I was standing was a table. Just to the right of me three large Mexican women were sitting there watching me and eating tortillas. To the left was a sink, a small cooker and a cupboard, a small kitchen equipped with plates and mugs. Standing by the sink stood an unusually pretty young girl, and just behind her, from another room hidden by a curtain over the door, an older woman came in. She seemed about ten years or so older than me with shoulder-length curly hair, wearing colorful clothes,

"Hi, we've been expecting you. Bring anything to smoke with you?"

She smiled and came toward me radiating warmth. I was a bit confused, and it must have showed.

"We've just seen you on the 10 o'clock news. You are the girl from the boat, aren't you?"

The mystical image of a clairvoyant that had floated into my mind subsided, and I smiled.

"I'm Bridget."

"Well welcome, I'm Rosie, the longest residing resident here. This is Susie," she said, indicating the pretty girl by the sink. "She is just starting her seven-year stint. The others," she glanced at the women at the table who were starting to move, "are just passing through. Would you like coffee or tea? Sorry there is nothing more exciting to offer you."

As we talked, she put on the kettle. Rosie was an American, a grandmother in her early forties. She lived near Ensenada with her boyfriend, growing vegetables and raising goats and chickens. She had been arrested with a small amount of marijuana, less than a quarter of an ounce, and had been here almost a year, still waiting for her sentence. Susie, only nineteen years old, was arrested with half a joint and had been there four months. Both of them expected a seven and a half year sentence, apparently the minimum for any drug offence. I wondered how many years I would get for two tons: maybe twenty, I contemplated. I fought back the thought. The other women had only been there a couple of days and probably wouldn't be there much longer; they were there for fighting, petty theft and prostitution. There were women in and out on these offences daily, Rosie explained. She and Susie had their beds in the far room and had it decorated with posters and photographs. Rosie had a television. She let me know that if I was going to be there for my sentence, they would make room for me. The other women went to bed, and Rosie and I talked while Susie sat and smiled and asked the odd question, speaking only a little English. It felt good to be sitting talking to another woman again, and I found myself verbalizing the sadness that had come over me in the dinghy as we tried to sink the boat: that now I would never know motherhood.

"Don't despair yet," said Rosie. "Try to get moved to Tijuana. I hear you can live with your boyfriend there. Just tell them you're a couple when and if you get there. They have restaurants and a park and dances."

"In the prison?" I asked, not believing what she said, thinking she must be mistaken, but not forgetting either.

Tiredness was finally getting the better of me, and Rosie sorted out a blanket and some sheets for me. I crawled onto a mattress with them and finally drifted off to sleep, wondering how Charles was and hoping he had been greeted as equally warmly as I.

The following morning I woke early. I lay there under my blanket not wanting to wake up until we all had to get up for a roll call. Two women guards came in. They joked in Spanish; my brain had been through too much, so I made no attempt to understand but asked permission to make a phone call; I was told, later. I stuck close to Rosie, thankful for her presence. The three large women were again at the table eating. A bowl of pinto beans was sitting on the stove. They took half of them and mashed them up with a half pound of lard and ate them with fresh tortillas they had sent out for. The old man, less awesome in the daylight, went to fetch things for the women. I borrowed money for cigarettes, and so the first day of my incarceration in the Mexican penal system began.

I had my suitcase to empty and my clothes to wash, so set about my tasks eagerly, glad to have something to occupy myself with. The first disappointment was that most of my better clothes, my chronometer, foul-weather gear and new underwear had all disappeared. Oh well ... I'd lost my boat, my freedom, nothing else could really make it worse. I set about washing what was left and hung it out to dry. I had a shower and then actually there was nothing else to do. I sat and watched: watched people with nothing to do fill their hours. The women passing through for a few days sat and ate the hours away. Rosie and Susie had both organized their own routine and, though smiling and friendly, in the daylight I could see the despair and sadness they tried to hide. The movie set disappeared and reality took over. I crept up to my mattress, climbed under my covers and cried. The tears gushed out, not noisily, just wetting my face and soaking the bed. They came and came; it seemed they would never stop. Weeks of built-up emotion and lost dreams all came tumbling out. Eventually after over an hour the tears subsided and I climbed out of bed into my new home. How could I pass two, five, ten or twenty years in this place? How could I keep my brain active, my body in shape, and my spirit alive?

I looked at Susie, an active nineteen-year-old girl: so much energy, so many hopes and dreams, so much to offer the world; would it all die in here? She changed her clothes frequently. She made clothes, pretty dresses and blouses, and would dress up as if she was going somewhere. She avidly read magazines and loved to look at pictures of faraway places, dreaming of beaches and islands in the sun. She asked questions of me, her eyes shining as she imagined the world outside. She ran around the tiny courtyard and used her jump rope incessantly. She danced and laughed, but at times looked so weighed down by sadness. She had a baby which was being taken care of by an uncle. He had a farm, and she liked to think of her little daughter enjoying the country, the smell of grass and the sight of animals. The uncle didn't approve of Susie but was giving her daughter a home, so she said nothing against him. Not being a mother then, I didn't fully understand how frightfully brave a person Susie was.

Every time anyone came to the door I requested an audience with the Governor. I wanted to phone England and phone the Embassy. I wanted to let my sister Judy know I was OK. It is such a helpless feeling to be locked up, to be at the mercy of someone else's whims. We watched Rosie's TV, which unfortunately could only get Mexican stations; at least I'll learn to speak authentic Spanish, I thought. We watched one soap opera after another. Their mainstay seemed to be long-drawn-out death scenes. There were no books. Nothing!

The following day was the same. Roll call, breakfast ... again I requested permission to make a phone call. Again no answer was brought back. Rosie was called and disappeared through the locked door. I missed her all day and just sat there. I can't remember a single period of my life just sitting around doing nothing. It was exceedingly hard for me. I sat and planned what I could do if only I could contact the Embassy. I was sure they could bring me books and papers. When were they going to let me call?

Rosie returned later in the afternoon. I could see she had been crying. It was her sentence. Although she had been expecting a seven-year sentence, I suppose there was always a faint hope a miracle would occur and she would be freed. But now that hope had gone. She had been sentenced, it was official, not just speculation any more. Her despair upset Susie, who was realizing her own fate. They both looked around their room, which would be all they would see, and the yard with its high walls, twenty-four hours a day for the next seven and a quarter years. How does one deal with that? I could not imagine how anyone could without losing their mind. The mood for the remainder of the day and the evening was one of gloom.

The old man brought in a couple of newspapers. Charles and I had made the front page. The photos the D.A. had allowed to be taken weren't for the files but for the newspaper. No wonder he had been smiling and sitting there proudly as our captor. The other newspaper had different photos: I can't even remember when they were taken, but it's astounding how unpleasant we looked. Tabloids the world over have a knack of making criminals look like people one definitely wouldn't like to meet. The accompanying stories were of course sensational and inaccurate. I was worried about contacting my family to let them know I was OK. I wondered how widely around the world the story would circulate. Would my family read about my fate in the newspapers, or would they think I had been lost at sea?

To an English person, the thought of a Mexican jail immediately conjures up a mental picture of dungeons, rats and torture; but although depressed, I had not been abused by anyone and it didn't seem that I was going to be. I went to bed that night with a heavy heart. Attempting to make positive plans about how to deal with my time was difficult when I wasn't even allowed to contact the Embassy or anybody outside who might organize getting me reading material, at the very least. I did decide I should start a strict exercise regime to keep my body fit. This was an easy decision to make after two days, but how would I feel after two hundred days, or one thousand days? Seven years are 2,557 days, and we would probably get an even longer sentence than that.

The morning dawned gloomy. I realized that much of the joy of life comes from waking up to a new day and new expectations, new smells and colors – the unexpected. That was all taken from us. There was nothing unexpected, no new stimulus, waking up was, for the first time ever, no longer a joy. I had every morning thanked God for a new day but now ... I prayed that today might be different and again put in my request for an audience with the Governor. I wanted to ask for visitation rights with Charles, a phone call to the Embassy and the return of my money so I could get something to eat.

Again Rosie was called out early, but she wasn't gone for long. She returned more cheerful, carrying some food. Her boyfriend had been. She said it was hard as they were allowed no physical contact, but he brought in fresh food for her and she, of course, shared it: burritos made with their own goats' cheese. She gave me one to send to Charles. Apparently, I later heard, it was devoured by twenty starving men.

Settling into another day, I was interrupted by a fat, cheerful guard calling me to come with him. I assumed it was finally my request to see the Governor being acknowledged. I walked back down those same dank corridors I'd entered along, what seemed a lifetime earlier. Getting back to the entrance hall, I was surprised and delighted to see Charles. Two men were standing there. The younger one yanked me around as I got near and put handcuffs on me. This was the first time it had happened, and I felt terrible. I looked at Charles: he had his hands tight behind his back, obviously with handcuffs already on. We were hustled out into a black van and pushed in the back.

"What about my money and my clothes? I don't have anything."

The younger man disappeared and came back with our

suitcases and the money I had given the old man. He climbed into the front of the van, and we were off.

"Where are we going?" we asked each other as we tried to shuffle closer together. The dark-haired younger-looking man had a brief discussion with the driver, and then he undid the handcuffs, leaving them attached to one hand only. He told us that we were being taken to Tijuana. He spoke slowly, going to great pains to make us understand. He said we would like it at Tijuana. Was this a prison he was recommending? We were so happy at that moment to be outside of that dreadful prison and to be together again and driving to Tijuana. I excitedly told Charles about what Rosie and Susie had told me about being able to live together in Tijuana. Charles was skeptical, but I remained hopeful. We shared our experiences of the last few days. Mine, I discovered, were somewhat better than Charles's. His first night he had spent in a cell 12 by 20 feet with eighteen other men. He'd had to fight them to stop them from stealing his clothes and money. The following day he was moved to another cell where long-term prisoners were kept. There was no food or mattresses, just cement and cardboard.

Relaxing in the van, we looked out at the ocean. How beautiful it was. The waves were rolling in from across the Pacific day in and day out, and of course were totally untouched and unaware of the changes in our lives. It was comforting to be reminded of its constancy and know that it would still be there unchanged when we finally regained our freedom, whenever that would be. The two-hour trip seemed to be over almost before it had started, such a contrast from the previous two days when each minute lasted an hour. The guards both began chatting amiably to us, sharing their sodas and potato chips.

"We're approaching Tijuana now; we'll be there in about twenty minutes."

I felt my body tightening up again. The next stage of our

journey was about to begin. The van slowed down and we stopped outside a large stockade, a high yellow wall with an orange stripe and barbed wire along the top. Heavily armed guards were patrolling the top of the wall. This was La Mesa State Penitentiary, Tijuana. We were driven through a heavy-gauge chain-link gate, which led to a small reception yard. How long would we be here? How many years and months until we were free? Fifteen? Twenty?

CHAPTER TEN

THE STRANGE WORLD OF LA MESA

Once we'd passed through the main entrance, we arrived at a row of bars about ten feet in front of us, through which we could see a raucous crowd of men and women peering and calling out. Behind them was an inner courtyard and a medley of colorful strange buildings. It was totally alien to any image of a prison that had ever passed through my mind.

We were taken to the left into a yard which acted as a kind of reception area. Here, our suitcases were checked before being handed back to us. There were no medical checks or physical searches. Immediately ahead stood a scruffy-looking whitewashed building which seemed to be a guard house. Armed guards came in and out staring at us up and down as if we were strange creatures from another planet. The guards wore uniforms of beige trousers and tan shirts and looked as if they had been selected for their physical prowess.

We stood there feeling lost, confused and disorientated. Out of the blue a guard appeared and led Charles away. I tried to tell the guard we were together and shouldn't be separated. He replied harshly, "*Espera*," meaning wait. Now alone, I continued standing there in the yard nervous, frightened and doubting the stories I had heard in Ensenada about couples being able to share a cell together. Feelings of despair were once again beginning to suffuse my mind. A bear-like gray-mustachioed man appeared. He was not in a guard's uniform, but a guard signaled to me to follow him. I followed him to the left clutching the handle of my suitcase tightly as if for security. He led me through a gloomy passageway between a mix of dilapidated buildings constructed of clapperboard, stucco and concrete. These buildings contained offices, commercial workshops, a couple of apartment complexes, shops and more. We came to another barred gate with another armed guard sitting by. He began to unlock the gate as we approached. In the corner, to the left of the guard, was a telephone booth with about four or five men standing around. My despair lifted slightly; perhaps, I thought, I would be able to use the telephone and call my family. I followed the man through the gate and heard it clanging shut and bolted as it was locked behind us. We turned to the right and looked down a long, dusty yard. On the left was an eighteen-foot-high thick wall topped with barbed wire; armed guards wearing knock-off Ray-Bans patrolled the walkway along the top of the wall and looked down on the men, women and children below. At each corner of the wall stood a watchtower, and there was another one in the centre of each wall. There seemed to be a lot of people wandering around. Maybe it is a visiting day, I thought idly, my brain all but numb with fear. We walked past a small kiosk selling food and drinks which was opposite a small restaurant. Passing between the kiosk and restaurant we entered a small square surrounded by apartments. Steps led up to a second floor with a balcony all around. Women were sitting watching children running and playing; the place seemed, under the circumstances, surreal.

He led me to a door in the far left corner of the courtyard. Above the door was a scruffy sign that read ominously *Tanques de Mujer*, the women's tank. He opened the door which led into a small room decorated with plants and colored crepe paper; to the right was a bunk bed and another opposite the doorway. To the left were a sink and a small cooker. Across the room was a curtain beyond which we came to three more bunk beds. On one of the bottom bunks a young blond girl of about twenty-two, dressed in a bright green and pink skirt with a white peasant blouse, smiled up at me, a gold tooth flashing as she did. She was talking to a couple sitting on rickety chairs by her bed. The man was smartly dressed and grinning. He looked like an Italian film star with his neatly groomed moustache. The girl with him was holding a baby of about fifteen months; he looked like a happy boy and had oriental eyes. There was a dark, long-haired girl reading a comic on another bottom bunk. The man with me mumbled something to her and signaled to me to put my case on the bunk above her. Having done as I was told he signaled for me once more to follow him. We went back out into the courtyard, this time turning to the right. We passed rows of hanging clothes and large washing sinks with three or more women hard at work washing clothes and, surprisingly, a couple of younger men probably aged eighteen or nineteen washing clothes too. To our right was a row of little apartments.

At this point the man I was obediently following called out to another older man to join us, and as he entered the first apartment he signaled to me to enter too. I learnt that the man leading me around was named Daniel. His friend Mario spoke excellent English and introduced him to me, explaining that Daniel was the *cabo* or head of the women's tank section. Daniel had assumed that I didn't speak Spanish, so he'd brought Mario to translate. I sat on a chair while they sat on a bed next to me. On the floor were two dark-haired boys, whom I learnt later were Daniel's sons; they were watching cartoons on a colour television. Whether I had any money seemed to be Daniel's principal concern. I had seven or eight dollars, but no, they needed $150 or I would have to do *tallacha*, which meant clean the section for two months to earn a sleeping mat. I quickly learnt that prisoners are expected to pay for their living expenses. Basic food would be provided by the prison, but everything else, the use of a bed, clothes and medicine, the prisoner would have to pay for themselves. The cost for a bedroll on the floor of the women's tank was about $30, $50 for a cot and $150 for a bunk bed with a curtain around it, which is the option I decided to go for.

Those unable to do *tallacha* or pay for a bed would have to sleep outside or in stairwells. I explained about my money, which had accompanied us to the judge in Tijuana. I showed him the receipt I had from the Captain of the gunboat. The large numbers, especially the 40,000 Italian lire, worth $40, impressed them, so I was allowed to owe it to them. I didn't worry too much about paying them as I felt that as soon as Jim realized our predicament he would give us the necessary funds for whatever we needed. How wrong can you be?

My interview was over, so I returned to my bunk and started sorting out my clothes. I had no sheets, but that didn't seem important and I was glad for the curtain around my bunk. The other occupants kept smiling at me, and I began to feel less afraid. The couple introduced themselves as Blanca and Fernando; they were doing seven and three quarter years. The little boy belonged to the blond girl, Maria, who was also doing seven and three quarter years. They asked me what I was in for, and when I told them they all agreed I would be in for a similar amount of time. They explained to me that I would need sheets, and a bowl for food and utensils. Food was brought around three times a day. Blanca told me that for breakfast we were given a roll, oatmeal and coffee; a roll and soup for lunch; and a roll, beans and coffee for dinner. If I wanted anything else, there was a supermarket and plenty of food kiosks to buy food and drink from. At that moment, I heard a clatter outside. Food was coming so Blanca gave me a bowl and a fork. Three young men were in the courtyard with two enormous pots, one filled with pinto beans and the other with chili beans. I had a large bowl of chili beans, which tasted delicious. There was no dining room, so we squatted down on the ground against a wall to eat.

When food was finished, a young man came to fetch me back out to the yard by the reception area, next to the main section of the prison. I was told to wait. On a bench, a skinny blond-haired man was sitting. I looked at the drawn, gaunt face for a few seconds before recognizing him as Charles with his hair cut and clean shaven. I rushed to him and hugged him, relieved to see he was okay.

"I didn't recognize you. What happened?"

"Oh, they dragged me off first thing to some barber who shaved me and cut my hair. It feels decidedly strange. I can't remember when I last had no beard. How are things going?"

"OK, it's such an extraordinary place it's hard to get my head round it, but everyone is being exceptionally friendly. I'm in a room with four others, and they are helping me. How about you?"

"Oh, the work *cabo* is letting me sleep on his floor. He has a house with two rooms and a kitchen. He says he'll be out soon, and we could buy his place."

"What, he has a house? He owns it? How much would it cost to buy?" I fired the questions rapidly at Charles. It seemed that Charles had discovered more about the prison than I had.

Officially named El Centro de Readaptacion Social de la Mesa, El Pueblito, Tijuana was built in 1956 on a 4-acre site as a municipal jail with an inmate capacity of 600. At the beginning of the twentieth century, Tijuana city was little more than a mud hole. At the end of WWI the town had fewer than 1,000 inhabitants, but prohibition drove US tourists there for booze, gambling, brothels, boxing and cockfights, causing Tijuana's population to balloon to 180,000 in the late 1950s. Migrants from southern Mexico poured into the town looking for work or a way to cross into the US. With continued growth came severe social and environmental problems. Many of these migrant workers falling foul of the law found themselves housed in this new prison, and they were allowed, as a new experiment in corrections, to have their impoverished families join them. Wives, children, girlfriends, even entire families would live inside the prison walls, some staying there full-time while others came and went at will. These families were allowed to build their own small apartments within the prison walls. The dwellings were known as *caracas* and came in varying sizes and levels of luxury. The prisoner would pay a certain amount of money to the jail to be allowed to build a *caraca* and sell it on when they left with a cut to the prison authorities. With the emergence of the billion dollar drug trade, many of the *caracas* built were quite luxurious with their own patios, equipped with sunshades, terrace furniture, barbecues and plants.

Charles and I sat and swapped stories about this strange place. Charles told me that as we were new we would not be allowed access to the main prison for three days or to visit each other's sections. Not until after we had finished *gritos* (Spanish for scream). I felt alarmed: it sounded like torture.

Charles laughed at the look on my face.

"Don't worry; it's a way for the guards to know who we are and why we are here. They need to know who the prisoners are and who the visitors are. Apparently, if any guard allows a prisoner to escape, the guard himself must serve out the rest of the escapee's sentence. They can also question us if they want."

I did not like the sound of *gritos* at all.

As we were chatting an American woman passed holding hands with a pretty dark-haired little girl.

"I'll be by to see you later," she laughed over at us.

Soon we were taken into an office where we were fingerprinted and photographed. When this was over we were again separated and sent back to our own sections.

I needed something to read, so as I nervously made my way

back to the women's section unaccompanied I stopped at a little kiosk which sold secondhand books. The young man running it spoke reasonable English and chatted with me. He had been there five years and met his wife while a prisoner and they now had a little girl. He used to be a pilot, till he was caught with a planeload of marijuana he had been about to fly to Arizona. Now he ran the kiosk and gave English classes twice a week. He gave me a book on flying, the only book in English he had. I also bought a notebook and decided to keep a diary to retain a sense of time passing.

I went and sat in the courtyard feeling relaxed. A young man, small and grinning wildly, probably in his late teens, came up to talk. Was I married? Was I lonely? After we had dealt with his opening lines, he was quite sweet. He told me about "Mama," an American nun living in the prison. He described her as an angel.

I returned back to the women's tank feeling pleased with myself for having been so adventurous. Maria was there having put her baby to sleep. She asked me how I was and did I need anything. I told her that I was nervous about the *gritos*. She smiled and told me not to be.

"Mama will be there," she said, "to make sure the guards behave."

"Is this the American nun I have just heard about?" I asked.

"She's an angel from God," Maria replied.

The following morning after a surprisingly restful sleep, the best I'd had in a while, I was called for *gritos*. When I arrived, Charles was already standing in a line of prisoners. I joined him, standing by his side, and as we waited the American nun arrived and started to walk down the line of waiting inmates. I watched her, intrigued after what I had heard. She was tiny, just five foot two, and wore a black-and-white habit and a crisp white veil which framed her beaming face. As she walked down the line of prisoners she gave a warm smile to all, and stroked each one's hand; she seemed not to notice if one was dirty, misshapen or unattractive. Occasionally she would stop and say a few words to a prisoner whom you could see was then warmed by her glow. As she approached me, I could see she had clear white skin, round cheeks and blue eyes where her smile seemed to begin. She came to me and Charles and greeted us warmly. Charles, a true Scottish Presbyterian, had an ancient distrust of Catholics but she smiled laughing at us and succeeded in getting a smile out of him. "I heard all about your adventures, what a marvelous story! I hope to read it in a book one day. Talking of which, here are a couple of English books to read." She handed us both a couple of books, mine by Agatha Christie. "Now is there anything that I can do for you?" I told her that I wanted to contact my sister Judy in London, and she wrote down her number and told me not to worry: she would contact my sister soon and would see us later.

The *gritos* then began. I had to walk between the rows of guards shouting out my name and crime repeatedly. I was supposed to say "Lane *contra la salud*" (against the health) but I didn't know and went down the line saying "Bridget, marijuana". The guards were allowed to question us, and a couple of them asked how much marijuana I was caught with. They were not aggressive to me, but I felt sorry for those arrested on less acceptable charges and the innocent. The guards could push prisoners or insult them if they wished.

Sister Antonia would stand there and try to give the inmates the courage to go through it while discouraging violence from the guards. I was told that there was a time when some of the guards would hit out at certain prisoners, and Sister Antonia would ask them to hit her instead. "If you feel the need to hit someone, please hit me. I am strong, and I don't mind. Don't hit that poor man, he is so weak; and do you know it's a terrible way to start the day. If you start it off hitting people it will make you feel awful all day and will eventually make you ill."

Apparently the guards started to stop the violence and went to Sister Antonia and said, "You know, Mama, we feel better."

When the *gritos* were over we passed back to our own sections and I went back to bed, still physically exhausted from our ordeal of the past few months. I spent most of the day reading; it was many years since I had read Agatha Christie, and I had forgotten how well she wrote. My roommates sat around playing cards a lot, and I played a few rounds of Twenty-one with them for *pesos*. The Sunday was our second day of *gritos* and we saw Sister Antonia again. She said she hadn't phoned my sister yet but would when she went over the border to San Diego on Monday and would bring us more books.

Sundays were visiting days in prison, and there was much activity. Charles managed to come over to see me, and I showed him my "tank". We sat at the little restaurant having a glass of milk and watching the bustle of activity around us. The pretty girl we had seen the first night as we waited to be fingerprinted came over.

"Hello, I'm Claudia. Sorry I have not been to see you yet, I will. This is my daughter Gabriella. It's her fifth birthday today, so please come to her party. It will be held in the main prison so you will need a *permiso*."

I looked down at the little girl's thick, light brown hair and beautiful face with enormous brown eyes, dressed in a frilly pink party dress. I attempted to wish her a happy birthday in Spanish and Claudia laughed. "She lives in the United States so speaks English." With that, the two of them rushed off.

THE STRANGE WORLD OF LA MESA

Sister Antonia

We got a *permiso* to cross over to the main section of the prison, and I got my first look at the place. As it was a Sunday and visiting day it was teeming with life; it felt like being in a bustling Mexican village, with children running and shouting, a jukebox blaring from a restaurant, young men sitting playing their guitars and others with their radios turned on. Craftsmen were trying to sell their wares to visitors, and a visitor had set up an umbrella and placed a cooking pot over a fire in the courtyard to make and sell tamales. Charles and I looked around at this hive of activity in astonishment.

The prison surrounded a large, dusty square where soccer or baseball was played every day except visiting day. Small houses, apartments, shops and restaurants surrounded the main square. A general store had a hand-painted 7-Eleven sign hanging outside it. In one corner were a school and library; the opposite wall had an enormous mural painted by an inmate who won his freedom for the work he had done. Behind the square were the large tanks where the inmates who couldn't afford individual apartments had their cells. There were a few bunks in each. Everywhere were small apartments, and way in the back, past a group of little restaurants, was the church. Sister Antonia had a carpenter's shop and yard close by the church where some of the men worked and lived. There was also a large hall being prepared for a dance, but it was also used for a gym, cinema and for award ceremonies. Outside the gym were a lot more workshops, a welding shop and an art shop. Looking across a basketball court was another row of houses with more shops and a row of raised chairs with shoe cleaners hard at work. Totally amazed, Charles and I made our way to the women's section where the party was taking place. There was a large colorful *piñata* in the shape of a rooster hanging in the courtyard. A *piñata* is a papier-mâché container that is filled with toys or candy or a mixture of both, and then smashed apart by hitting it with sticks as part of a celebration. Lots of kids were running around the *piñata* playing excitedly. Cake and ice-cream were being served to everyone in the section by Sister Antonia and an older grayish man of forty odd years. He was about five foot eleven, with a lined face, vivid green eyes and a moustache. I assumed he was a helper of Sister Antonia's as she introduced us.

"Arturo, you must meet Bridget and Charles. They're the ones we were reading about in the paper."

Later, as the party was finishing, we sat with him. Arturo helped Sister Antonia, but he was an inmate, nearing the end of an eight-year sentence for drug smuggling; he was also the Nicaraguan woman Claudia's boyfriend and one of the most important people in the prison, respected by inmates and guards alike. Sister Antonia was telling me how she wanted Arturo to open a doughnut shop to help raise money for the poor in the prison. Poor prisoners who were too sick to work and had no relatives or friends on the outside to help them had a hard time surviving in the prison. They were reliant on the likes of Sister Antonia and charitable donations.

Charles, Arturo, Claudia, Sister Antonia and I sat and talked and, unexpectedly, joked for a couple of hours. Sister Antonia then had to leave to visit the hospital in Tijuana. Before Arturo, Claudia and Gabriella left to go to Arturo's *caraca*, he offered to arrange for Charles to spend the night with me. But the idea of crowding into that small bunk in a room full of others was not what we wanted, so we declined. After they all left we sat in one of the restaurants on a manic thoroughfare known as the "Boulevard of the Eagles". We drank a glass of milk and tried to come to terms with the reality of our crazy new home and just how long we would be there.

CHAPTER ELEVEN

A HOME OF OUR OWN

Monday 1 June 1981 was an eventful and busy day for us. It was our last day of *gritos*, our first day in court and our first night in our own *caraca*. We also received official notification of the charges against us. We were charged with possession, introduction, transporting and trafficking marijuana. We were unprepared for the court appearance, since we had been given no warning of it and knew not what to expect. My own image of court was the Old Bailey in London where judges wore wigs and there was a formality and order, and you would know what to expect.

Early in the morning after our last *grito*, we were called to the reception area and put into a van to be driven through the gates and out into the streets of Tijuana. Blanca and Fernando also had a court appearance for an appeal they had in motion. This was of some comfort to us as we didn't feel so alone. The trips to court became the most depressing times for me. I had slowly learned to adjust to life in our small prison village where we were free to walk around. But on trips to court where we passed down streets we weren't allowed to walk on, and saw people we couldn't talk to, the loss of freedom was reinforced. After driving through the Tijuana streets, we arrived at an attractive, low white building clad in pink bougainvillea with colorful flowers growing in front. We were all hustled out of the van and marched through the garden to a cell where a heavy door was opened, and we were all pushed in. It was dark inside and other men were already there squatting against gray walls carved with initials and messages. Eventually everybody chatted amicably. We sat in a dark, damp, stinking cell for most of the day, smoking heavily. In a poorly curtained off corner was a badly plumbed smelly toilet covered in flies and stained heavily with urine and feces.

At one point, Charles and I were called out to see a lawyer. To me in my mind, he resembled a greasy little weasel and he wanted us to hire him. He grabbed my hand telling us fervently to say we didn't know that the marijuana was there. I tried to explain to him that we were not averse to lying for our freedom but to pretend that we hadn't noticed two tons of marijuana in a 40-foot boat when we were way out at sea was not credible. The lawyer didn't understand and obviously thought we were crazy.

We had put in a request for the public defender, but as yet had received no reply. When we finally went into the courtroom, it was an office with a couple of men wandering in and out and a secretary typing. It was similar to the room where we had given our initial statements in Ensenada, so Charles and I just gave the same statements and left. At that time, we had no idea that this was our court appearance, the one in which the judge would decide our fate. There are no trials by jury in Mexico. The judge decides the case and sentence based on documents and statements presented.

We were returned to the dirty, damp cell and had to wait a few more hours until the van arrived to take us "home." We arrived back at the prison tired and too late to eat, but Arturo and Claudia invited us to dinner with them in their *carava*. Arturo's two-year-old daughter, who lived with him in the jail, was already in bed asleep. Their apartment was upstairs overlooking the main square. It consisted of a kitchen diner, a bedroom, a bathroom and a spacious living room with a large color television. It was tastefully furnished and paintings hung on the walls. It was easy to forget we were in prison with such entertaining hosts and in such a pleasant apartment. They had a pet, Pepe the parrot, and there was a young Indian boy, Aftab, in his late teens, who served us burritos and tacos followed by fresh fruit salad and cottage cheese bought at the local restaurants.

Arturo showed us a *caraca* next door to his that was coming up for sale. It was a spacious apartment with a kitchen off the living room which had a balcony overlooking the square, a bathroom with a hot shower, and a bedroom with windows where you could see beyond the prison walls. We loved it; Arturo said it would cost about $30,000. Maybe, I thought, hopefully, Jim would get it for us. I still had faith that he would help once he knew where we were. Charles looked skeptical.

Arturo also owned the nicest *caraca* in the women's section for Claudia to use when he left. He said Charles and I could use it for now and accompanied us back there, first clearing it with the guards. That night we slept together in our new home, a room which seemed exceptionally large to us with its fridge, bed and bathroom with a hot shower. We were overwhelmed. It was unreal waking up together. In the morning, Arturo had arranged for fresh bread to be delivered to our door, followed by breakfast. We had our first relaxed day. I wrote in my diary, "A small space to be on one's own makes a huge difference."

We were directly next door to Sister Antonia's *caraca*. Hers was a little 10 foot by 10 foot concrete room with a cot as her bed, and with a Bible and Spanish dictionary on a small bedside table. A large crucifix hung on one wall, and a few photos stood on a small table alongside a large jar of peanut butter. She kept this so that she was always able to offer something to eat to any hungry prison inmate who might knock on her door. The only sunlight in her tiny cell filtered through two small windows that had a view of a guard tower and a barbed wire fence. A white sheet served as a door to a cramped bathroom with a cold-water shower.

A HOME OF OUR OWN

Every evening, once we moved into our new room, Sister Antonia would stop by before going to sleep, perch at the end of our bed and glowingly tell us about her day. On her first late night visit to us, she told me she had talked to my sister Judy the previous day, and that I had a new niece, Francesca Maria, now seven months old. She admitted telling Judy that I would need money, despite my having told her not to. I felt relieved to know my family at least knew I was safe and not lost at sea. Slowly, Charles and I began to settle into the daily life of the prison: a prison run like a little village, a village we couldn't leave.

La Mesa was unlike any prison I'd ever heard of. No one except the guards wore a uniform. The director of the prison was a political appointment, and an important appointment because, in addition to his salary, from a low operating budget he was also allowed to draw off money from the internal prison economy. His main role appeared to be to contain the prisoners, keeping them alive and peaceful. Under the director were four commanders, one of whom was always on duty at the prison. Under the commanders were the guards, and a few clerical workers. The administration's main concern was security. The escape rate was impressively low. Any prisoner who was considered a security risk, regardless of his affluence, was contained in the solitary confinement cells known as *tombas*, or in the Corrall, four two-storey tanks surrounded by a high chain-link fence. The punishment cells, the *tombas*, were called this as anyone put in them felt they were being buried alive. They were a miserable row of cells, each measuring about 5 foot by 10 foot, each with a heavy door and only a tiny slot for light and ventilation. Here, any prisoner caught for any infraction could be incarcerated for varying amounts of time. The Corralls were also kept locked, and the men crowded into them. Both the Corralls and *tombas* were dreaded by everyone, and there was considerable sympathy for any one enclosed within them.

SAILING INTO THE ABYSS

Provided by the government was the prison area, the tanks and three meals a day. There was an infirmary with two doctors and a nurse in attendance. There was also a school which had a couple of outside teachers come in, although most teachers were inmates. Against the costs that were accrued by the government was the percentage they got from all businesses operating within the prison and the sale of houses.

Beyond making sure no one escaped, the guards were also in charge of collecting a percentage of the payments from the various *cabos* (prisoners who were heads of different departments). These were from the sale of beds, blankets and apartments and for upkeep and the use of showers, as well as cuts from the various businesses such as restaurants and workshops, run inside the prison. A few guards also made extra money on the side by procuring or turning a blind eye to illegal goods, such as drugs or alcohol. This apparently was not as widespread as it had been in the 1970s when the prison housed a lot of Mexican drug kingpins. After a big shoot-out in 1978, when the then prison director Salvador González and assistant director Jesús Domínguez Cobos were murdered, a forceful crackdown on organized crime in the jail was initiated. The drug kingpins were all moved to various parts of Mexico, at which point apparently the jail changed and became less violent and corrupt.

Most of the bigger houses and apartments had been built in the days when La Mesa housed the drug kingpins. They lived in luxury and carried on their operations in the prison while smaller houses were built by other inmates. An advantage to owning your own *caraca* was that you had the key and the guards did not, so the residents locked themselves in at night. The tanks were not terribly comfortable: the older ones had dirt floors and in the men's section was a congested warren of cells, but they provided shelter and they were not locked up except at night, so inmates were not forced to sit in idleness all day long.

Searches occurred fairly frequently, usually around midnight when everyone was asleep. We would hear banging on the door and would have to get up to let the guards in who would then search everything thoroughly; it was a frequent reminder that we no longer had control over our own destiny.

Anyone caught in a criminal act inside the prison would have another charge against them. One young teenage boy was serving twenty-one years for less than a quarter of an ounce of marijuana. Initially he was given seven years for possession of a joint, but later he was found with a small amount on him in the prison so he got another seven years, and then finally his girlfriend tried to smuggle in a small amount for him but was caught and thus received another seven years and his girlfriend also was sentenced to seven years.

The two important times of the day were 6 a.m. and 4 p.m.: these were the times for roll call and everyone had to be accounted for. Other than these formalities the inmates were left on their own to work, lounge or play. Some inmates spent hours gossiping, gambling with dominoes or cards for petty stakes or just strolling back and forth across the prison grounds.

The prison routine was broken by visiting days on Thursdays and Sundays, which frequently created a carnival-like atmosphere, especially if it was a festive holiday. Prisoners were allowed to receive as many visitors as they wished and the visitors were free to mingle in the prison. Shortly after we moved into Arturo's *caraca*, Fathers' Day came around. It is an important day in Mexico and falls on the third Sunday in June. There were 1,200 inmates in La Mesa at that time. That day, 2,000 visitors, entered the prison. There was music, bands, dancing, skateboards, and people selling everything. It was difficult to believe in that carnival-like atmosphere that we were in jail until we looked up and saw the high barbed-wire walls and the watchful armed guards.

SAILING INTO THE ABYSS

Conjugal visits were allowed on Tuesdays and Fridays, but could only really be taken advantage of if the prisoner owned or had access to a *caraca*. But they represented a fundamental part of the humane aspect of the Mexican penal system. The conjugal visiting rights for all prisoners meant there was not the problem of homosexual rape prevalent in United States and British prisons. Apart from the administration and security, all other work was done by the prisoners.

Our attempts to see the Public Defender were not getting us anywhere. We had filled out forms applying for our money but heard nothing back. Having no money was becoming a problem.

On 21 June, I received a surprise visit. I was called to the lawyer's visiting rooms and presumed it was at last the public defender. But instead it was a lawyer hired by my brother and sister Judy. He arrived with much needed money, and asked if we had found anywhere in the jail we wished to live. He seemed to know intimately how the prison worked. I told him of the apartment next to Arturo's and said I thought it was too expensive. He just asked for details. He also said he would get hold of our papers in the court and when he had read through them would be back to see us.

Much to our delight the following day we were informed by the *cabo* of housing in the main prison that the apartment was ours complete with furniture. On 22 June, we moved to our new home. I wrote that day in my diary, "I've never lived in such a comfortable place, space is such a luxury, walking around from room to room, sitting at a table having books and magazines around to look through, looking out and seeing beyond the walls, the mountains, the border, the airport, cars ... my own front door."

We were visited the following day by the British Embassy; Mr Whitton arrived from Mexico City. Embassies cannot do much for foreign prisoners. They cannot give legal advice, intervene in court proceedings, provide funds to pay legal costs or fines, get a person out of prison, or obtain special treatment for them in prison. Mr Whitton explained all this to us but wanted us to keep in touch, telling us that we could phone reverse charge any time with any problems. He said that he had notified my father and was trying to contact Charles's sister.

I wondered how my father had reacted to the news of his eldest daughter being locked up in a Mexican jail as a drug smuggler. Little did I know that the same day he received the news that he was being presented with an award by Margaret Thatcher, the then British Prime Minister, in recognition of his contribution and services to British industry. I had always striven to be a daughter he could be proud of, and now felt I had let him down.

My father shaking hands with Margaret Thatcher

CHAPTER TWELVE

PRISON POLITICS

Three days later, after moving into our fabulous apartment, I passed my 32nd birthday in the prison. Two large cakes were brought in to me. The prison rock group serenaded me with "Happy Birthday" in Spanish and English, and people popped in to see me all day long wishing me "*cumpleaños feliz*" (happy birthday).

Charles's birthday was a week later, and I cooked him eggs and bacon for breakfast, one of his fantasies out at sea. In the evening, I cooked him a festive meal which we shared with friends.

We had been in La Mesa barely a month, and it seemed so much had happened and we had so much to assimilate that it was quite exhausting; added to that was the weakness of our physical state when we had been arrested. Slowly we began to recover and got to know more people and shops and restaurants of our new neighborhood.

The prison had its own bakery, and the baker, an inmate, was so gratified by my enthusiasm for his fresh bread that he delivered it to our door every morning. The basic prison food was delivered down to the women's section door to door, but in the main men's section they had to queue up for their meals. There were no restrictions on food brought into the prison by friends or relatives though all was subjected to a thorough search. Then there were restaurants serving all kinds of Mexican food and sit-down restaurants where prisoners could have a splendid meal of chicken or steak. There was a barber, a hairdresser and shops selling different kinds of produce, a supermarket selling tins and packaged goods and a butcher's shop. There was a variety of small food kiosks to choose from, making delicious fresh fruit salads with cottage cheese and honey, marvelous milkshakes, fruit popsicles, tamales, sandwiches, and tacos. Fresh flour tortillas were also sold at kiosks, the best made by a man sentenced for poisoning his wife. There was even an ice-cream parlor. As Charles and I sat one day eating ice-cream and watching a soccer game, I noted in my diary, "It really is a total movie. I wish I could sketch all the little houses with the numerous TV aerials, a veritable toy town. It seems that if someone kicked the ball too hard it would knock them all down."

Slowly, Charles and I began to adapt to our new life. Charles got a job working in the kitchen; he enjoyed it and it meant we had a food allowance. The kitchen workers were granted small apartments in the kitchen, and they got an allowance of eggs and vegetables as their payment. The kitchen was run totally by inmates. It never ceased to amaze me when I visited the kitchen that they had all these gruesome-looking knives there. But none of them were ever used for anything other than for cooking purposes, and there were no guards needed to guard them. The work also helped toward Charles's "good time." With good time you could leave after serving two-thirds of your sentence, there not being a parole system like in the United States or the United Kingdom.

I started exercises and playing volleyball, going to the gym each morning at 7 a.m. with a small number of other women. Few women bothered to go to the exercises. The instructor who came in from outside eventually gave up coming, as not enough women showed up. In prison you have to keep pushing yourself, as it is too easy to slip into lethargy. Later on, exercises for the women became compulsory.

In my time there, I was first involved in teaching English, helping an American girl Cynthia, also in for marijuana, in the school in the women's section. Unfortunately, they were so used to hearing American English that they found my British English too hard to understand. Cynthia was a large girl with the most beautiful face, large eyes and extremely good-natured. As a moving-in present for our new apartment, she lent us a small television. I then began helping in the prison's pre-school. A Montessori teacher came in from outside to instruct interested inmates how to teach children. A San Diego-based group called *Los Niños* donated materials such as powdered milk and peanut butter, so the children would have snacks. I was impressed with the enthusiasm the children and their parents showed.

From the balcony of our apartment, it was just like looking down on an English village green, only it wasn't green but brown: there were people playing football or baseball, kids running around, people strolling or standing in groups talking.

Sitting out on my balcony, I had a lot of time to observe the prison and think about the whole system. I was brought a copy of the *LA Times* one Sunday and read an article about Folsom State Prison in California. It reminded me of the horror of British prisons, violence, rape, wasted years turning out bitter people unable to adjust to the outside world. In the early 1970s I had become involved in the prison reform movement in England, and had visited a couple of inmates who had no visitors. The whole experience had been depressing, and I hated what imprisonment did to people. But at the same time there were people from whom society needed to be protected. Here in Tijuana I saw something closer to what an ideal prison should be, though by no means perfect: a place that protected society and rehabilitated inmates by allowing them to keep in touch with the positive areas of their lives, such as their families. One of the most important factors was the extraordinarily liberal visiting policy. In these contacts quantities of food, clothing, and money were allowed to be given to the inmates.

PRISON POLITICS

This in turn developed a market system out of the barter of these goods, allowing the purchase of bedding and special sleeping quarters, and the operation of stores, restaurants, and kiosks. Thus, it mimicked the social realities outside the prison and forced the prisoners to make daily economic decisions. As in real society, a prisoner's wealth, industriousness and bartering ability determined what food he ate, his living quarters, dress and social status. Men who were skilful at bartering were admired, whereas the drug addicts who sold their gifts from their families for a pittance were despised, just as in the real world.

Prisoners could also get work in the commercial workshops that operated inside the prison. Several private enterprises leased space within the prison, supplied the necessary materials and paid the prison a fixed price for each item produced. These companies paid the prisoners a fixed wage. The workshops produced articles such as carved wooden furniture, tambourines, bongo drums and miniature carved ships. The downside to these workshops was that the prison also took a "service fee" known as a *mordida* from the workers' pay checks. I felt this money earned by the prison should have been put back into the prison. The sanitation in the prison was old and antiquated and left a lot to be desired. The money could also have been used to help the old and sick, among others. No one in the prison was required to work, but if a prisoner had no help from friends or family bringing him food or money, the economic demands of the prison would force him to seek employment, again mimicking the real world.

Despite being in prison for whatever crime, a man or woman could have their whole family to visit; they could continue to be a parent to their children, a husband/wife to their spouse and a son/daughter to their parents. They could earn money in prison and help support their family. They could have their family stay awhile, look at their kids' school work, and talk over problems with their children, all the things a parent should do. This was not only beneficial for the prisoner, but also for their family, who were so often the innocent victims of penal laws. Kids need parents, they do better in their presence, and suffer when the relationship to a parent is severed or breached.

In the US and UK and many other countries around the world, when a man or woman is imprisoned the children who have committed no crime are forced to pay a steep price. Too often, much of what matters to children—their homes, their safety, their public status and private self image, their primary source of comfort and affection—is robbed from them. In the US and UK, the focus of locking someone up is the deprivation of love and touch. The way to disempower people is to strip away all human contact. Although the deprivation is intended for prisoners, this aspect of punishment also falls heavily on their children. Whatever sentence is passed upon a parent, the child will serve with them. This frequently leads to children ending up in reform homes, the start of their own path to prison.

In the US, among the things judges are explicitly barred from considering in their mandatory sentencing laws are the needs of children. Mandatory sentencing laws in the US have helped make women prisoners the fastest growing segment of the prison population nationwide. A woman is sentenced to be away from her kids and her family. Children are sentenced to be without their mothers or fathers. Today the shocking number of three in every hundred American children has a parent behind bars.

Many spouses who had elected to live with the inmates in prison on a permanent basis would leave the prison on Monday morning for work. Juana, who was one of my first English students, worked at a factory in Tijuana making suitcases. While she was at work, her husband Antonio looked after the children in the prison. Every evening she returned to the prison and joined the long line of other permanent visitors waiting to have their bags of groceries checked by the guards and have "permanent visitor" stamped on the back of her hand. This regime allowed the family to be kept together as a unit.

One of the things I noticed early on in La Mesa was that, apart from at the *gritos* in the first three days, people were not known for their crimes. They were the baker, the doctor, the telephone man, the postman ... the TV repair man. In fact, the TV repair man was one of the most important men in the prison. Everyone had a TV; most of them were old and cheap so always in need of repair. He took on some younger men as apprentices, teaching them his skill. It was interesting to see that everyone did something to earn money, and so crime (while we were there after the big clean-up of the 1970s) was virtually non-existent. One Sunday I watched an older man with a makeshift cart put up a little notice: "Rides around the yard, 5 pesos a child." On visiting days, he was busy all day long, his cart filled with laughing, happy children.

The inmates with more money, such as Arturo, gave jobs to the poorer ones. Arturo had Aftab, the young Indian boy, to act as a babysitter for his two-year-old daughter and to run errands. He had someone else to do his laundry. The women mainly did laundry and sewing to make money. A crowd always congregated by the main entrance to run messages, such as to tell when lawyers arrived, or visitors were there, and they would get 5 or 10 pesos per message. Whatever your skill you could put it to use, and more importantly you could discover a new skill. There was even a prison music group that provided music lessons.

The school had a couple of teachers coming in from the outside, but it was mainly run by inmates as many prisoners were professional people; so the younger men, mostly street kids who were very often illiterate, attended classes and learned to read and write.

SAILING INTO THE ABYSS

Sport in the prison was extremely important, especially soccer. There were eight teams within the prison. These teams had their own league but also competed in the Tijuana league, so outside teams would enter the prison to play. Charles played enthusiastically for two different teams during his imprisonment. The baseball team, known as the *Tigres de la Mesa*, also played teams from outside the prison.

Basketball and softball were the other main sports, but boxing and volleyball were played too. Archie Moore visited the prison on a few occasions to encourage the boxers. Sometimes in the evenings Charles and I would sit on the balcony and watch the young men kicking the ball around, and we realized that for some of the young men it was the first time they'd had a chance to relax and be kids. They gained some self-respect by having the chance to show they were adept at something. We knew a young man, Raimond, who had been treated as an inferior all his life, but he turned out to be proficient at softball and his whole self-image changed. Another young man they called *Changita*, little monkey, who did the washing for Arturo and was picked on by the others, became a truly talented boxer. I always remember the look of pride on his face as he won a bout one day.

Charles in goal during practice

PRISON POLITICS

The prison ran as a community, and I had rarely lived in so peaceful a community anywhere else. It was more representative of life on the outside than most institutions, so the adjustments were not as dramatic. The pressures and temptations which often led to crimes, such as lack of work, drugs and alcohol, were at that time virtually absent. Everyone had somewhere to sleep, and something to eat, but the possibilities were there to do so much more. Although I saw many negatives, on the whole I felt that the system was one of the most humane I had ever come across, and one that the US and UK penal systems could learn much from.

Not only did the prison allow whole families to visit, they also allowed many visitors from the US who brought skills or simply love. Sister Antonia was one of the first, having visited the prison since 1965. Twelve years later she made the prison her home. She brought many other people to the prison, some of whom came regularly. Noreen Walsh and Mary Jasper we met in our first week. They would bring magazines, clothes and food, and we always looked forward to seeing them.

One weekend, Dr Merrel Olesen came to the prison with his wife Marie. Sister Antonia had met them in San Diego. Hearing he was chief of plastic surgery at Scripps Clinic, she told him about the prisoners' tattoos and how much having them removed would enhance their chances of finding work and acceptance on the outside. Dr Olesen set up a crude clinic in the infirmary and, with Marie and Sister Antonia to aid him, started to spend one weekend a month removing tattoos. The list of those wanting them removed grew and grew. One day crossing the yard Dr Olesen noticed a young man standing in a group. He had a cleft lip which disfigured his whole face. He asked Sister Antonia about him and arranged to do surgery on the lip. When Cesar saw himself after the surgery he cried, and when his mother came she stared at him, afraid to ask whether it was truly her son. I saw him afterwards, so much more self-assured. Occasionally Dr Olesen would bring other doctors so that they could see more prisoners during a visit. At times I cooked dinner for them, and enjoyed their company considerably.

Others too visited the prison. Jerry Miller was a woman from Pine Valley who had been visiting La Mesa for twelve years. She had gone the first time with a friend and had been struck by some of the young men and women, not any older than her own children. From that day she had returned once or twice a week bringing magazines, candies, clothes, any little thing to improve the quality of life of some of the poorer prisoners. Each month her husband accompanied her, and they showed films and cartoons in the gym. Rusty Whittaker, another San Diego woman, would visit the prison and hand out flowers in the main square.

The prisoners appreciated the visitors, and they were all treated with respect. For the visitors too there were benefits. Their understanding developed that when you treat people well they tend to behave well. It often amazed me that while a large majority of crimes for which people were imprisoned were crimes of violence, murder and rape, yet I rarely saw any signs of violence. It is true of prisons throughout the world that most inmates are not mentally disturbed psychopaths. Luckily these tend to be a tiny minority. The majority were street kids hardened by years on the streets filled with drugs, alcohol and violence. In La Mesa at that period of time, they lived and worked together peacefully. There were always children everywhere, and the children had a humanizing effect on the majority of people.

One of the most valuable things Sister Antonia tried to teach people was that she did not live with murderers, rapists, and drug traffickers; she lived with poets, doctors, carpenters, men and women from all walks of life. She loved to quote Nathaniel Hawthorne's story of "The Minister's Black Veil." The minister wore a veil and everyone wondered what great sin he had committed, but he would never say. Finally, on his deathbed, his words were to this effect: "Behold, before each countenance I see a veil. We have all sinned, but not all have had their sins made public. We do not introduce ourselves as liars, fornicators, blasphemers, so why in prison should everyone be known for their worst sin."

I considered myself extremely fortunate and blessed when Sister Antonia asked me to become her secretary. I considered it a great honor to work alongside such an extraordinary woman. I was kept busy as I slowly worked through box after box of unanswered mail from the last five years. I answered them and started to write a quarterly newsletter about her activities and life in prison.

Working alongside her, I discovered the fascinating story of Sister Antonia's previous life, a life that would normally have barred her from becoming a Catholic nun.

CHAPTER THIRTEEN

AN ANGEL OF GOD

The epitome of all the positive energy within the prison was the "White Angel." Sister Antonia Brenner was a divorced mother of seven who had lived her life in comfort in Beverly Hills, with a summer house in Laguna Beach. She had always been deeply aware of the oppressed and the poor and involved herself in charity work. She had visited the prison fourteen years earlier with supplies and had never forgotten it. After her divorce, when her children were grown up, she applied through Bishop Maher of the Diocese of San Diego for special permission to join the Sisters of Mercy. She moved into La Mesa with no Mexican papers and speaking no Spanish but with love in her heart. She believed love would conquer all, and it is astounding what she achieved with love as her only weapon. She said she had a self-imposed sentence to live in jail.

We heard horror stories of what the prison used to be like: it was once the toughest, most notorious jail in Mexico, and she moved in when it was like that. She had no fear, and even when confronted with a man toting a gun or knife she would smile at him with genuine love and ask for the weapon. Not once was she ever refused. She says in all her years in prison she still has not met anyone bad. She likes to tell about the man in the punishment cell who had been involved in violence and drugs all his life and was considered a truly evil man, but with her he was always gentle. One day he said to her: "You know, Mama, you think I'm so good, and you know, Mama, you're right; I have such beautiful thoughts. But you know, Mama, they think I'm so bad, and they're right too. I'm cruel and I'm evil. I'm all those things. What I am, Mama, is the wood; and you are the carpenter."

I felt very privileged to spend so much time with her and get to know her so well. She joked that she used to look at all her unanswered mail and look to Heaven and pray for a secretary, and then I arrived. Although appreciating my help, she prayed for our freedom as fervently as us. During our time together we enjoyed working with each other as we felt an immediate rapport. She saw her daughters in me, and I saw my mother in her. I had been raised a Catholic, though it had been many years since I'd attended any church service. My basic faith in a loving God remained strong and to me Sister Antonia was my ideal of a person of God, unlike the Evangelicals who entered the prison talking of damnation and carrying their bibles like guns. She told me once that her ambition was to reach the stage where she judged no one. It was one of the main things that made her loved by the prisoners, her non-judging, her total acceptance of them as they were, asking nothing of them, no guilt, no explanations, just their love.

The prisoners called her "Mama," and it was that special mother's love she gave them. She called all the prisoners and the guards her children. She told me that she'd heard that touch was very beneficial for health; and in that case, she said, her face radiant, "I should live forever as I'm touched and kissed continuously, all day long." It was true. I'd watch her cross the yard, which took me a matter of minutes; it could take her over an hour. Men and women would crowd around her and her hands would go out in every direction to try and touch as many people as possible.

One day we woke up to a great commotion. Claudia explained that "Name Days" in Mexico are as important as birthdays, and for Antonia's day there was a tremendous weekend celebration which began in the evening in the women's section with a band playing.

SAILING INTO THE ABYSS

The woman guard on duty joined in the dancing: first she danced with one of the women, then she danced with one of the young men, and finally she danced alone. Other prisoners and guards clapped and sang. A crate of soda arrived. After a couple of hours the band left, and everyone slowly retired to their beds and slept.

The following day was totally devoted to Sister Antonia, and the love felt for her by everyone in the prison was evident. Mass was planned in the main square at 12 noon, Mexican time. The boxing platform had been brought out and was decked with masses of flowers of all colors. A bouquet of red and yellow roses had been sent from the Administration. Musicians appeared again, and Sister Antonia climbed up onto the platform. The trail of children disappeared under the platform to play in the shade. After the mass a festive meal was cooked and fed to everyone; meanwhile Sister Antonia took a large cake off to the *tombas* to feed those prisoners first.

Yet another celebration was planned for later that evening in the women's section, and after that some ex-inmates were going to take her out to dinner in Tijuana town. At 8 o'clock that evening another cake was brought out. This one was covered with white cream and pinkie cream roses. After more smiles, more songs, more photographs, she took this cake to share with the guards, who all loved her too.

I tried to see her at least once a day. It was easy when we lived next to her, but when we moved to the main section it was harder. So often when she was on her way to see us, she would get waylaid and diverted off elsewhere. She liked to visit the men in the *tombas* every day. She was working hard to get the *tombas* abolished. She hated cages and couldn't understand why people wouldn't see that if you locked someone up like an animal they would become like an animal. She wanted to help the inmates overcome the past that had got them there and knew that treating them like people would be a first step. She believed in the system in La Mesa, thinking that living inside in the same manner you would live outside gave the prisoners a better chance at rehabilitation. She did succeed in closing down the *tombas*, and the Administration gave her the space to open her own St Joseph's Carpentry Shop. New punishment cells were built, however; but Sister Antonia never ceased campaigning against them and did all she could to bring comfort to those locked up.

After every trip to San Diego Sister Antonia returned to La Mesa with her car filled to the top with clothes, books, shoes, food... She'd drive into the yard and I'd help her unload, sort the items out and distribute them. One day I helped heat 150 burritos she'd been given, a treat for those in the *tombas* that night. She always saw the positive side of things. Sometimes, some of the inmates would get new blankets or clothes and sell them. I was with her one day when one of her "sons" complained that Roberto had sold the blanket she had given him to Jose. "That's good," she smiled, "so now two people are happy. Jose is warm, and Roberto has some money."

She also took food to the police stations where prisoners were remanded and weren't normally fed before being sent to jail. She visited the families of the prisoners. I remember her returning one night extremely pleased as a family who had disowned their son when he was arrested had promised to visit him. She had gone to tell them not to be ashamed of him as he needed their support. She told them to think of all his positive qualities because these hadn't changed with his imprisonment. They came to visit him the next day, and I watched them embrace warmly

Every morning after the *gritos* Sister Antonia liked to share a morning prayer in the little church. I sometimes went down to join her, enjoying the quiet, informal get-together in the church. I was with her on the third anniversary of the prison's big shoot-out when eight men had died. Sister Antonia remembered them in her prayers and reminded the men that we continually have to choose a path to take in our lives, but that because we sometimes take a wrong turn it is no reason we can't regain the right path. We must not live in the past but for today. Everybody likes to look forward, yet so many people continually harp on whatever crime brought the prisoners in, turning guilt and revenge into virtues. Sister Antonia's attitude was refreshing.

One of the men from Charles's soccer team was staying with our neighbor. Sister Antonia told me one day that he'd spent three years at a downtown Tijuana jail, a terrible place where people were thrown haphazardly into cells like dungeons. He had no medical training but had worked in some capacity for the Red Cross. He turned his tiny cell of 6 feet by 6 feet into an infirmary and cared for all the older inmates, using bandages and medicines brought by Sister Antonia. Even the guards learned from Sister Antonia, and the easy rapport between guards and inmates seemed strange when we were first there; but it was just another of those things she had been responsible for.

One morning there was a young man who simply could not handle the *gritos*. Something touched him and turned him inward, and he became virtually catatonic. An inability to handle the *gritos*, however, was disobedience and must be punished, so he was dragged off to the *tombas*. Sister Antonia accompanied him. Outside he sat stiffly, seemingly unaware of anything while Sister Antonia tried to comfort him. Knowing he should not be in the *tombas*, she got permission for him to go to F Tank instead. F Tank was where the disturbed men were put. Arriving at the door, Sister asked the guard who was taking the man to treat him well.

"Of course, Mama," the guard answered, and continued looking at the man, smiling. "We'll look after you; everything is going to be fine. A big tall man like you will be OK here. Do you play basketball? I bet you play basketball. I bet you play basketball real well, a big tall man like you. You'll probably become the star basketball player. Yes, you're going to be fine..."

As he continued, slowly the new inmate responded. The unexpected kindness, the thought of another person caring, resulted in the new man entering F Tank smiling. The guard grinned around at a delighted Sister Antonia. "You see, Mama, there are two methods I can use: my fists or my head," pointing at each. "I prefer to use my head. How much better a world it would be if everyone used their heads."

When inmates entered the prison charged with certain crimes, Sister Antonia liked to be there because she knew that the other inmates could sometimes be cruel. A woman was brought in charged with killing her seven-year-old son. Sister Antonia came to fetch me. She wanted me to help the woman through *gritos*, and as I was following Sister Antonia, I was thinking: "What kind of awful woman is she?" Reaching the woman's section, I looked at the woman: a year younger than me, seven children living and no husband. Her face was painful to look at, as it contained so much sorrow. How could anyone judge her? Sister Antonia talked to all the other women; had they never hit their children? She showed them that the woman needed their support; no one could make her feel worse than she felt herself.

She saw good in all situations. One of her "sons" named Maharis escaped one day from the hospital in Tijuana. His guard had fallen asleep, and Maharis had walked straight by him out the door. Very few inmates escaped, and the guards were extremely angry with him. Sister Antonia knew that they'd find him, as she knew he wouldn't be able to resist going to his mother's house; so she talked to all the guards, making them see how praiseworthy it was that he'd escaped without hurting his guard. It had been a risk, as if the guard had woken up while Maharis was walking out he could have been shot in the back. By the time Maharis was rearrested, the guards were proud of him instead of angry.

Sister Antonia hated cells. She said they made good men bad and bad men worse. She also hated the concept of punishment. She believed very strongly in the healing powers of forgiveness. She started a Day of Forgiveness on Ash Wednesdays. She asked everyone to write down the names of those they had harbored grudges against and then collected them all. There was a Mass in the main square and Sister Antonia collected all the bits of paper and took them on to the altar and burned them. She then used the ashes to bless everyone, including the guards. Many prisoners told her afterwards that for the first time in many years they felt free; free from the hatred that had been festering within them for years.

Sister Antonia liked to have money to give the men when they left prison, because so often they were released late at night with nothing and nowhere to go. One of her dreams was to have somewhere for the men to go. One evening she came to see us, very excited. "I have a room. I'm calling it The Room on the Second Floor." She had been given a room where the men could stay for a night or more till they had got themselves sorted out – a halfway house. The man who had given them the room was going to try and find jobs for them also. She had been with me only ten minutes when the usual interruption came, a young man called Carlos. "Mama, I'm leaving. I just wanted to say Goodbye." "Where are you going, Mijo?" asked Sister Antonia. "I don't know, Mama. It's too late to get a bus to my home town. I'll find somewhere to sleep, Mama."

Sister Antonia looked round at me, her exuberance radiating from her face. "You see," she said to me, "it's so marvelous." Then putting her arm through Carlos's arm, she said, "But Mijo, I have somewhere for you to go." And off they went, arm in arm.

She also wanted a house for women, which she would call the House of Martha and Mary, an alternative to the bars and brothels (*cantinas*) of the red-light district, which was the only place so many of the women felt at home in and would return to on their release. She told me about Diana, one of the women in the women's section. I never liked Diana much, not for anything she had ever done, just her general demeanor. She smoked constantly, twitched as she moved and had a nervous tic. Her main problem was that she'd never fitted in, and even Sister Antonia admitted that she'd had a hard time loving Diana when she'd first met her. She told me about one evening when Diana was asking for her boyfriend. She was worrying he would not come to spend the night with her and started demanding that Sister Antonia should go to fetch him. She went to Sister's *caraca* to tell her, and Sister Antonia explained she could not do that. Eventually Diana said to her, "Mama, if he doesn't come, will you do something for me? Will you come to my tank and sit by me till I go to sleep, because, Mama, I don't want others to know I'm afraid of the dark."

Poor Diana; I realized that many of these women only knew the sexual touch; when they wanted warmth and friendship the only thing they could do was find a man. Where else could women like Diana go but the *cantinas*? The Christian community, the respectable community, didn't want her.

The other person I met who wouldn't fit in and of whom Sister Antonia was thinking of when she talked about her House of Martha and Mary was Paloma. Paloma arrived in the prison a couple of weeks after us. The first time I saw her was when Sister Antonia brought her into my *caraca*. We were still in the women's section. We heard Paloma's story of how she was actually a boy but unhappy in her body. She felt herself to be more a girl than a boy. Her family were horrified and said she would bring disgrace to the whole family. So she was told to leave the house. She was taken to a bar in Acapulco, where for three years she was sold to men. One day a man paid money to take her and another child to a motel. When he got them away from the bar, he let them go. She got a job washing dishes and was happy till someone recognized her and told everyone she was in fact a boy. Thrown out again, she went back to the bars, the only place where she was accepted. She went to Los Angeles and worked the streets with another transsexual until her friend was murdered. One day she met a genial man called Ken and they fell in love. But Paloma, afraid of his rejection when he discovered the truth, ran away. Ken found her and asked her to go with him. The others in the bar laughed: "Paloma! That's no Paloma, that's Mario. He's a man."

Paloma couldn't look up, but Ken didn't leave.

"Come on," he continued, "I don't care, I love you."

With his support she decided to have the sex change operation and then get married. It was while in Tijuana that she was arrested for something petty. She was, in fact, innocent of the crime. For people like Paloma there is no place in our society, and so Sister Antonia dreamed of her House of Martha and Mary.

When Sister Antonia was away from the prison, she was badly missed. Her own real birth children told me that after a day away their mother couldn't relax, worrying about her "children." Time moves at a different pace when one is confined. A day is a long time. Sister Antonia understood that, in order to do all she did for the prisoners, she had to be away sometimes. I knew that when I regained the freedom I prayed for every day, a part of me would always be with her; glad that, despite everything, I'd had a chance to meet a truly remarkable human being.

CHAPTER FOURTEEN

LAWYERS AND LAWYERS

Our lives at the prison continued. Charles carried on working in the kitchen; he enjoyed it. I settled myself into my new home and rarely ventured forth. Helping Sister Antonia became a full-time job, and she brought me a typewriter and filing cabinet.

Interspersed with daily life in the prison were certain strange occurrences. We had accepted the Mexican lawyers who had paid for our *caraca* and were hired by my brother and sister. One day an American lawyer appeared, smart and, I confess, easier to believe than the Mexicans. He claimed he had been sent by my Family, emphasizing "Family" as if he didn't actually mean family. I was confused. I wondered if maybe Jim was finally doing something to help us, but the lawyer was asking a lot more than he was telling me. He wanted to know all about our Mexican lawyers and what they were doing, but told me not to mention him to them. After he left I felt acutely paranoid. A week later he came back with another man. He was still acting as if sent by the Mafia, and we certainly meant different things by the use of the word "family." I was more cautious this time, and felt the second man was angry with how little information I was prepared to give them.

A month later another strange incident occurred. An American couple were brought in on unspecified charges. The wife, Veronica, was out on bail within a day, but she and her husband—known, by various names: Ross, Pat and Edmund—came to make friends with us. Veronica told me how she wanted to help Sister Antonia and asked me what was needed. Ross sat around trying to talk about "dope deals we have done" and coming out with comments like "We probably know lots of the same people: drop some names and I'll see if I know them."

Our friends Max and Vera, whom we'd known in Panama, were coming to visit us. I wrote in my diary on 21 August of Ross, "My mistrust of him increases rapidly, especially since I discovered Max and Vera are coming to visit in their own car. Why is he so anxious to meet them?" I'd asked Ross, who had also by now got bail, to phone our friends and tell them how to get to the prison. He told me first that they were flying down, so he would drive them to the prison; then it transpired that they were coming in their own car, but he still insisted on them going to his house. Max and Vera had been such dear friends to us in Panama, totally unaware of what was really going on. Ross assumed they knew something about our trip and contacts, so tried the same clumsy techniques on them as he'd tried on us to get information. After this we saw little of Ross and Veronica; Veronica's philanthropic interests disappeared as quickly as they had appeared.

My life passed mainly inside our *caraca*: writing letters for Sister Antonia, as well as my own correspondence, occupied most of my time. I finally managed to write to friends I'd not had time to write to for years, and had never before had a permanent return address to write from. Now I had one though not of my choosing, and I would receive letters in return. I made yogurt to sell and planned on maybe opening a yogurt shop. I started by selling it in the kiosk, in the women's section which Claudia had started to run and had doubled in size after Arturo had gone free. I never made any money though, and the planned shop never happened.

Days would come and go fairly monotonously and time passed interminably slowly. The male inmates went jogging around the main square every morning. I wanted to jog also, but didn't want to do it alone; whereas Charles got all the exercise he needed by playing soccer. On 27 June I wrote in my diary: "Living in a boat certainly trains one to adapt to a lack of space, however, the endless sea and sky compensate, here the endless noise and concrete will soon tire the mind."

Occasionally there were days that were noteworthy. On 15 September the Queen of the Penitentiary was chosen. The women spent all day with their hair in curlers, choosing their best clothes to dress up in. Finally Nieve, a pretty, slender girl of twenty-two with short brown curly hair, was chosen as Queen. She was crowned on a platform in the main square by the Director of the prison. She was wearing a long pink evening dress and fur-lined cape. Two other girls were chosen as her princesses, and they also had long glistening evening dresses. Their scars and tattoos disappeared as the pride shone from their eyes, and they walked with a new dignity. The Queen's prize was to go and let most of the men out of the *tombas*, and everyone cheered.

Then 24 September was the Day of Mercedes, the patron saint of prisoners. All night long there was singing and a candle-lit procession. For the two days previously there had been building going on in the main square: a crude cattle pen had been erected. The children were quick to use it as a new play area, and the men sat around on the wooden bars wearing large cowboy hats. On the morning of the 24th a truck drove into the prison and deposited three horses and six bulls. They paced around the pen while Mass was said. After Mass the fun began: the first spectacle was of the male prison inmates attempting to ride the horses. The third horse was extremely frightened and tried to climb out of his pen. When anyone tried to ride him, he kicked out wildly. Finally, he was subdued and blindfolded, and the rider mounted. The horse had lost his enthusiasm for everything, not wanting to move despite being hit and goaded. Suddenly fed up, he leapt up throwing his rider to the ground, trampling on his face and kicking wildly until he was brought under control and moved out of the ring. The crowd loved it. The rider was hurt and stunned but lived to tell the tale.

Next came the bulls. There were men riding them and playing at being matadors; some of the bulls were friskier than others, and without warning would charge and create excitement among the spectators. Some of the bulls seemed bored by the whole spectacle and wanted nothing to do with the humans who were trying to provoke them. Nobody succeeded in riding them for long. Between the horses and the bulls some children, nattily dressed, performed clever tricks with lassos, proudly twirling their ropes around. The whole prison seemed to be watching, guards and inmates alike; every balcony was filled, and people also stood on the roofs to watch, a true spectacle. Once finished it was back to the monotonous roll call and the bull ring was dismantled; nothing was left but a memory.

Searches continued on and off. The first rains came, and we found we had leaks. As householders, as on the outside, we had to repair them. Charles had to get permission to go on the roof to check out the damage, and then we investigated what would be the cheapest way to repair it, taking into consideration that we could not wander into a hardware shop to buy what we needed. We ended up using our next-door neighbor who had access to decent prices on hardware. We paid for the materials to repair our roof and the neighbor's roof, while he did the work for free.

Another Sunday I heard reggae music for the first time since leaving Bequia the previous November. It came from the basketball court. I looked over and saw a large crowd. I wandered over to see what was happening. Peering through the crowd, on a small makeshift stage, I could see a mass of vivid color: reds, yellows and blues. A limbo dancer slithered under a pole amidst spirited encouragement. It was Ron Road's Caribbean Ensemble, which consisted of ten dancers in bright, exotic costumes with a steel band. An unexpected pleasure: apparently one of the dancers knew an inmate, who asked permission for them to perform. The Administration was happy to comply as long as it cost them no money or time and benefited the prisoners. The audience loved it, and the musicians and dancers reacted to the enthusiasm.

I tried to earn some money making decorations for a Swedish girl in San Diego. It was a lot of work for extremely little money, but our expenses were low with Charles working in the kitchen. If we hadn't got help from my sister and brother, we wouldn't have had our *caraca* or lawyers and life would have been very different. The only response I'd got from my request for help from Jim was $500. A second letter from Jim had arrived saying we had got ourselves into "this mess" and should have dumped the cargo. I answered trying not to get too angry, pointing out certain facts such as that he had not once suggested that in our conversations, and I didn't think he or his Colombian partners would have appreciated being told that we had dumped their cargo. The letter was answered by a card saying a parcel was on its way. Sister Antonia was hoping it was full of money. She arrived just before Christmas excitedly clutching a parcel. It had to be checked, so the two of us watched while the guards opened it. It was a Harrods gift box from London containing tea, rum butter and cookies; a delightful box but, considering he'd given us nothing else for all our trouble, it felt insensitive, a mockery. I was actually less disappointed than Sister Antonia, having already faced up to the fact that he'd totally let us down. Against that disappointment was the joy of having so many friends who'd rallied round to offer help, and the total support my sister and brother had demonstrated.

The year continued slowly. I can't remember a year taking so long to pass since I was a small child. In October I began feeling nauseous, moody and tired, and then one morning I discovered lumps in my breasts. I went to the prison infirmary and saw the American woman doctor. "I want to do a biopsy," she said, calling to the Mexican doctor in charge of the clinic. He looked at me: "Could she be pregnant?" he asked. "I suppose so," I answered, thinking at the same time that it might explain my irrational behavior.

The next morning I submitted a urine sample and proceeded to wait. It was six long days before the results came back. I was handed an envelope with "Congratulations" typed on the outside: I was pregnant. Sharon, the doctor, immediately started talking about abortion and how she was afraid it wouldn't be possible. I looked at her. Maybe she was the sane one, and I was crazy, but I was thinking it would be lovely to be pregnant, even though I was facing an eight-year prison term. I went back to my *caraca*, not sure how to think or feel. Later that evening Sister Antonia turned up.

"Have you heard anything yet? she asked eagerly.

"Yes, it was positive. I'm pregnant."

"Oh, how marvelous. What a lucky baby to have such wonderful, loving parents."

Charles and I looked at each other and finally admitted to ourselves and each other the joy we felt at the news. I started to read everything written about pregnancy. Friends in the United States and Britain sent me books. It became the focus of my life.

Thanksgiving came, an American holiday celebrated on the fourth Thursday of November, and I thought back to my last one so full of hopes and dreams in Puntarenas. Arturo was already free, and he brought in the thanksgiving turkey along with all the trimmings. We had a party in our *caraca*; nothing was missing—only wine, but that didn't seem to matter. Claudia had just discovered she was pregnant, and we celebrated her joy. Our babies would be born within a few weeks of each other, and we would be able to support each other through our pregnancies.

LAWYERS AND LAWYERS

My friendship with Claudia was a deep one. There are not many situations in life where you live so closely with someone, sharing similar experiences twenty-four hours a day. Even in a family, you all go in different directions during the day. Claudia was a Nicaraguan girl who had been arrested with cocaine. She had been studying in the United States where she lived with her young daughter Gabriella before her arrest. She had already served a year before we arrived. It never ceased to amaze me how cheerful she always was, despite her separation from her daughter, which caused her great pain. Gabriella had lived with her for a time in prison, but Claudia felt it was not a healthy environment for her as she grew older. She still visited for long weekends and for special holidays. I too worried about having a child in prison, but there was the continued hope that our lawyers would get us out. Claudia helped everyone, letting women use her *caraca*, lending them money and clothes. She had spent time in Europe and loved to talk with me about London and her time there. She had met Arturo in La Mesa.

Arturo's background, as a Mexican–American brought up on the streets of Los Angeles, couldn't have been more different from hers. He'd been in and out of prison all his life. He was self-educated and had an inexhaustible appetite for knowledge. He taught himself chess while in solitary confinement in a US prison so he could pass his time there playing chess games in his head. I tried to play a mental game with him but failed to retain as many moves in my head as he could in his head. He was a very ethical man and loved to have long philosophical arguments with Sister Antonia. He had his two-year-old daughter from a previous relationship living with him, and he was a devoted father. Because of his relationship with Claudia he carried on living in prison after his release. They were no longer our neighbors as Arturo lost his *caraca* when he went free, so they moved over to the women's section. He was free to come and go, and so he sometimes brought in special food for us all.

Another month and we were getting ready for Christmas. Being English I made traditional mince pies. We put up a little Christmas tree and decorated our living room. Friends put presents underneath our tree. Christmas Day arrived. Charles didn't want to get up to work and knocked over without seeing the stockings, filled with fruit and little trinkets, that I'd put up late the night before. After his shower he went to make coffee and still didn't notice the stockings. He came back to bed, so I went and fetched them, which put him in a better mood as he went to cook Christmas dinner for 1,200 inmates. When he came home, we opened our presents and then sat around while various friends called in to wish us "Happy Christmas." Sister Antonia's three birth sons came by with her. We sat and watched the children rushing around the square with their new toys. It was sad to be in prison away from my family, but it could have been a lot worse.

I did a lot of entertaining in prison and hosted many dinner parties. The only other prisoners I spent much time with were Claudia and Cynthia, but I also provided afternoon tea for all Sister Antonia's visitors. Four Sisters arrived from Northern California, the Servants of Christ. They came to work with the mentally ill in Tijuana. Two of them, Sister Adele and Sister Margarita, came to visit me once a week. I took numerous visitors of Sister Antonia's on conducted tours of the prison. Katy from Los Niños, the San Diego-based group that supported the prison pre-school, would bring young visitors down. I would accompany them around the prison. Katy arrived one day with a small group from Arizona State University. They were impressed with the prison, especially with the sports program. The boys decided they wanted to challenge the prison basketball team. The following day twenty-five extremely tall American students turned up, along with their own cheer-leading squad. The prison reacted by forming their own cheering squad.

LAWYERS AND LAWYERS

The Arizona State team won. They were twice as high as our team, but it was a great game and everyone enjoyed it. Our team invited the Arizona State team back for a rematch.

Sometimes Sister Antonia would ask me to accompany her to the gymnasium for an award-giving ceremony. The Mexicans loved awards. I went with her for the graduation ceremony. There were awards for those who had completed various courses: a high school diploma, reading... There were dancing displays, short sketches by the theater groups and many, many speeches. I found it hard to follow and would tend to drift off into my own thoughts, just watching the faces, the pride, the smiles and the laughter.

The Mexicans enjoyed parties and festive days. One of their most celebrated days was Mothers' Day. It was 10 May and Cynthia came to fetch me to go over to the women's section. As we turned down into the yard, I saw a large table with a three-tiered cake. When the women arrived each was given a carnation. The prison group was there singing "mother" songs. Goyo, the prison photographer and also an inmate, was there taking pictures. After a little speech about motherhood everyone was given a blanket as a present. Being eight months pregnant, it felt good to be called a mother.

Later in the day I went to the gym for the main Mothers' Day entertainment. There were lots of singers from outside, all dressed in black velvet dresses and plenty of lace. The whole show was being broadcast on the radio. A slinky lady with a sultry voice sang a sexy number and was a massive hit; a couple of the men got up and danced with her. Everybody cheered, and the lady responded well. In between numbers a clown played with the children, while men with sombreros serenaded the ladies.

These were the fun days. Then there were the endless days of boredom, when we would gaze out beyond the walls wondering when we'd be free. There were also the desperate days. The worst days were the days after a transfer. When the prison became overcrowded, a list of names would be forwarded from Mexico City: a seemingly arbitrary list of names, and a hundred or more men would be moved in the night and sent off to the Islas Marías. The Islas Marías was a penal colony situated between the tip of Baja California and the mainland. Life was very tough there and discipline harsh, but for most of the inmates the hardest thing was to be moved so far from their families. Dependants could move to the Islas too, but daily visits were not possible from the outside. Rumors would start circulating around the prison that a transfer was imminent, and everyone would become exceedingly nervous. The first anyone knew about it was the knock at the door and the guards escorting the prisoner off. You were not allowed to take anything with you, not even your trouser belt. The first time it happened we had heard nothing during the night, but the next morning I went out to pass my roll call. I felt the atmosphere, the heaviness, the sorrow. No one was jogging around the square; no ball was being kicked around the square. The groups of men usually engaged in animated conversations were now silent. During the day I became aware of certain *caracas* remaining locked, certain businesses staying closed, familiar faces no longer seen. In the sixteen months we were in La Mesa, there were four transfers. It never got easier, but along with the sadness was the thankful feeling that Charles had not been moved. We were still together.

Visits from the lawyers would either make me feel marvelous or plunge me into depression, but they would never leave me unmoved. We had two lawyers at first, Augustin and Felipe. They contradicted each other constantly and smiled as they gave us three or four opposing statements within the same paragraph. From the first, they insisted we'd be free within a couple of months, never saying quite how but suggesting a multitude of ways: "How far is the prison wall from your *caraca*?" Felipe asked one day. Augustin spoke no English so he would talk to Charles or just stand there mumbling away to Felipe, who carried on asking obscure questions and making extraordinary comments: "Do exercises, we need you to stay seriously fit, you might need it." Then they left. Were they planning an escape? All night we lay awake wondering. I had no intention of jeopardizing the health of my baby by attempting an escape.

We didn't know in those early days that Mexicans like to tell you what you want to hear, even though it has nothing to do with what is actually going on. All along we had felt that the only chance of being freed would be in pursuing the argument that we we'd been in International Waters and thus committed no crime in Mexico. This didn't appeal to them. They would simply assure us that we would be free soon and pat me on the head. They always treated me like an idiot, which infuriated me.

Sister Antonia talked to my sister Judy in England, who wanted to know how we were enjoying the color television she had paid for. Where was the color television? The lawyers gave us excuses for six weeks: "It broke just before bringing it to you." "It's being repaired." "We forgot it." "It's too large to bring in. The major won't let it pass." Eventually one day we were called to the gate, and there they were struggling with a 25-inch color television. "Your sister is arriving tomorrow," they told me. She didn't arrive, but as the lawyers believed she was going to, they got us the television.

Then they turned up with a third man, small and rotund. This was Gaston. I liked Gaston. He spoke good English and tried to make us understand what was going on, instead of Felipe's "don't worry your little head about that" attitude. They suggested we give a new statement about having had engine problems in the ocean and meeting another boat who said they'd go and get our engine part if we looked after their cargo which was animal foodstuffs. We agreed to this as at least it seemed more believable than claiming not to have noticed the cargo. We had to go to court again to give a new statement. This time, because I was pregnant and didn't want to be around all the cigarette smoke, I was allowed to sit outside the dank cell. It was strange to be sitting there watching people walking down the street and knowing that if I tried to join them I'd be shot in the back. The Judge objected to our changing our statement and some heated arguments went on between the prosecuting attorney and Felipe. I finally got to see the Judge when he came in; he looked at Charles and me, said we were obviously guilty and why were they wasting the court's time. With that he strode out. Charles and I felt gutted. Felipe said we weren't to worry. This was easier for him to say than for us to do!

I wanted to keep a calm demeanor for my baby's sake, and this was hard when dealing with the complicated legal performances. Sometimes the lawyers arrived late at night and once at two in the morning. They didn't realize the fear generated by banging on the door, waking us out of our sleep. Was this a transfer? Was it a search? They applied for us to be moved to La Paz and didn't understand how that frightened me. La Paz was a small jail like Ensenada without access to all the amenities we had in Tijuana, and at six months pregnant I didn't want to be moved.

Another time they neglected to file a particular paper, so we were notified we were being defended by the Public Defender yet again, not that we had ever managed to see him the previous time. One day a new lawyer arrived. He claimed he had been hired by the cousin of the man who was acting for my family. We met the cousin who was legitimate. We signed papers for the new lawyer Rosales, but explained to him that we did not want to exclude Augustin and Felipe from the case in case they really were achieving something. Rosales assured us he wouldn't, but after we had signed his paper he changed them. Next thing we knew there was a hurt Felipe needing us to sign more papers re-establishing his authority.

LAWYERS AND LAWYERS

On 30 March Gaston arrived with Felipe and Augustin in tow. They were immensely proud of themselves as they told us they had convinced the court that we were illegally arrested and going to be deported. Though excited, at seven months pregnant I was also extremely anxious. Nothing happens fast in Mexico, so they told me not to worry. Again that was easier said than done when I knew that immigration prisoners were always held at the dreaded downtown Tijuana jail. On 25 May we were sentenced to seven years and eight months with a 5,000 peso fine. I wondered how this fitted in with Gaston's claims. At this point it was hard for me to deal with anything, as my baby was due to arrive any day.

CHAPTER FIFTEEN

BORN INTO CAPTIVITY

The main thing getting me through the whole prison ordeal was my baby. Having arrived in Tijuana and realized that a baby was possible, the desperation I'd felt about never becoming a mother had disappeared. So when I had discovered I was pregnant it was a surprise. From that day on I concentrated on keeping fit and well.

One day in November, after a trying session with the lawyers, I noticed I'd been bleeding slightly. I took to bed, and Charles took over the cooking and cleaning as well as working. I concentrated on eating well and resting. I was so glad I'd managed to give up smoking. I started doing pre-natal yoga, and spending a couple of hours each day talking to my baby.

I was very unhappy with the infirmary's attitude. They took no medical record and seemed uninterested when I told them my blood was Rh negative. Being Rh negative does not affect your health except during pregnancy. A woman is at risk when she has a negative Rh factor and her partner has a positive Rh factor. The combination can produce a baby that is Rh positive. Although the mother's and baby's blood systems are separate, there are times when the blood from the baby can enter into the mother's system. This can cause the mother to produce antibodies against the Rh factor, causing the mother's body to treat the Rh positive baby as an intruder in her body. These antibodies will then attack the Rh positive baby's blood, causing it to break down the baby's red blood cells, and anemia will develop. In severe cases this hemolytic disease can cause illness, brain damage and even death. When this happens, the mother is said to be sensitized.

The medical staff tried to give me medication for my nausea, but I didn't want to take anything. I'd always hated pills and man-made drugs. In fact, I strongly believed that if marijuana was legalized and people could smoke a joint when tense upset or stressed, there would be dramatically fewer housewives addicted to tranquilizers and sleeping pills.

A very dear friend sent me a copy of *Spiritual Midwifery*, a book with glowing accounts of home births at a spiritual community in Tennessee. A few days later another copy was given to me by Sister Adele. Did this mean I should have a home birth? Claudia brought the Nicaraguan Consul doctor up to see me. Dr Roger Hernandez was an obstetrician who practiced in San Diego and in Tijuana. He took my medical record, which made me feel much happier; I sensed he was a good doctor, and I liked the way he answered all my questions. Sister Margarita told me she knew one of the Plenty Organization midwives, the same ones as were involved in *Spiritual Midwifery*.

Mary Fjerstad was one of the original commune members on the Farm who had traveled to Tennessee from Northern California in the late 1960s. She had left the Farm to go with her family and other commune members to live with the Indians in Guatemala. There she had taught them pre-natal and post-natal care as well as soybean technology. Because of her husband's problems with his knees, they needed to move to a drier climate and so came to San Diego. Mary wanted to continue pre-natal education in places where it was not available. She heard about the prison and said she was interested in meeting me. On 10 December she arrived. Mary was the same age as me, about 5 feet 4 inches tall with long hair and an open kind face with deep serene eyes that looked straight at you. She immediately made me feel at ease. She checked me over and assured me that I was doing well. She had brought her stethoscope, and Claudia and I got to hear our babies' heartbeats, faint and fast. It felt marvelous. I talked to her about a home birth as I had decided, after much reading that was what I wanted. Mary also visited the women's section and started giving pre-natal help to all the pregnant women. Finally, I was getting all the help I needed. Dr Hernandez took my blood to do all the necessary tests and planned to do a complete physical examination. When the bleeding stopped I started getting heartburn. Mary started her weekly visits, and they became really valuable to me as I felt so vulnerable and needed to be reassured. It was true for the other women too.

Charles and me in our apartment

Mary brought pre-natal vitamins for all the women. She checked their weight, blood pressure and showed various slide shows. There was a particularly inspirational show of a home birth. The reaction from the other women was more positive than I'd imagined, and for me, it intensified my desire for a home birth.

Claudia and I began to crochet baby clothes; it was fantastic that we were able to share our experiences together. Late in January

BORN INTO CAPTIVITY

I felt the baby start to move. I enjoyed lying in bed and watching little arms and feet make my stomach move. I discussed having a home birth with Dr Hernandez, who also approved and understood my reasons.

Normally, at that time in La Mesa jail, a woman who goes into labor was taken to the local downtown Tijuana hospital in handcuffs. I hated hospitals and also wanted Charles to be there for the birth. I started to become obsessed: I would not go to the hospital. Sister Antonia began to enthuse about the advantages of home births to the Prison Director and Infirmary Doctor, preparing the ground before I asked for permission. Mary taught Sister Antonia a few basics about child delivery as well, as to how to check my dilation so that she would be able to help. Claudia and I continued to crochet, and I tried not to worry about lawyers, as being stressed would start my bleeding again.

By the end of April the baby's head had dropped, and I began to get exceedingly anxious. I wanted Sister Antonia to check in on me all the time and panicked when she was away from the prison. On 4 May the Director gave his permission for me to give birth in my *caraca*. I relaxed a little and Mary brought in all the equipment she needed, sterile kits and her birthing bag. I was undergoing antibody checks every month because of the possible Rhesus problem. I had enjoyed being pregnant and had given it a great deal of attention, but now I felt I was ready for the birth.

Soon, 25 May arrived, the anniversary of our arrest; the day we received our sentence; so the same day, Claudia threw a baby shower for me. She had got permission to bring in a bottle of wine to go with the numerous tasty canapés she had provided. Arturo arrived carrying the food, a white cream cake covered with red roses and a gallon of wine. Manuel, a bank manager in on fraud charges, brought his guitar and sang. Everyone else arrived dressed up and wishing us well. I almost had a hangover the next morning; it had been so long since I'd drunk any alcohol. (It was in the days before drinking while pregnant was considered a danger.)

The baby shower

By this time, Mary and Dr Hernandez were checking me every few days. They thought I could go into labor at any moment, and it could be fast. The whole prison was excited, knowing our plans. On 29 May I had a few contractions.

On 1 June my due date arrived, and then disaster. Sister Antonia told me that the Director had withdrawn his permission for the home birth. I immediately applied to the Judge, but he answered saying he couldn't give permission to have a baby. It was an act of God. I tried to talk to the Director, but he would not budge and he let me know that all the guards had been told that if I went into labor I was to be taken to the hospital. I was devastated, furious and stormed back to our *caraca*.

"Darling, it'll be alright. I'll come to the hospital with you," Sister Antonia rushed after me trying to calm me down. Dr Hernandez followed her, also trying to reassure me. Charles hurried to see what was wrong as we all arrived at the *caraca*.

"They've changed their minds, damned Mexicans. I hate them.

They just think they can appease you by telling you what you want and then change their minds," I ranted. It was true. They all did it.

"What!" Charles roared. "No way, we'll deliver him by ourselves."

Again Sister Antonia and Dr Hernandez tried to reason with us, but I was beyond reasoning. "No," I shouted for the first time at Sister Antonia. "I'm serious about this. We'll barricade ourselves in. I won't go to that hospital. I'm having our baby here. We'll manage," and with that I slammed the door and threw myself on the bed. Dr Hernandez realized I was not going to change my mind so talked to Charles: "OK then. I'd better give you some lessons in emergency childbirth."

He ran through what should happen, what he should do and what he should watch out for; and what could go wrong. Luckily we had all the equipment already in our *caraca*. Everyone went, leaving us alone. "Are we doing the right thing?" I said to Charles, knowing that if he said No I'd be furious; but he looked at me and smiled, "You know we are."

The next day was a blur. Lots of visitors: Katy, Noreen, everyone had been told what was happening so all avoided talking about it. Mary appeared, and I explained what was happening. I immediately became defensive, assuming she'd try to change my mind. "You don't need to have anything to do with it; Charles and I are willing to do this alone."

"Bridget, hang on. I understand how you feel. I was just thinking it would be better if Dr Hernandez or I was there, so maybe we can help a bit."

"How do you mean? Of course I'd rather you were there."

"Well, you're two days past due date and the head has been engaged for weeks. At the Farm we never liked to induce births, but sometimes when the baby was ready but holding off coming out we'd help it. You could take some castor oil, and that might start labor. It might be worth trying tomorrow: you know it's visiting day and both Dr Hernandez and I will be here. I think I may have some in my bag." She looked and sure enough found some. "OK," I said, willing to do anything but go to the hospital.

I was anxious all night and then at six in the morning, straight after my roll call, I took my medicine. It tasted revolting. I wandered backwards and forwards for the next couple of hours and then … was that a contraction? Yes, labor had started; I was going to have my baby. Now all we had to do was prevent anyone else aside from Mary finding out. Charles sent a message to the kitchen that he had visitors so wouldn't be working, the first time he'd done that. We decided that he would have to keep people away from me all day. We were expecting Rusty, maybe Gerry. We didn't want anyone to know, as we didn't want to involve them. From my bed I heard people asking after me. "Oh, let me go and see her," I heard from Rusty's voice. "No, she's sleeping," countered Charles. My contractions were getting stronger and I wanted to be able to relax into them, but I was so afraid of making any noise that I tensed up. Nine months of reading everything written on pregnancy, on how to relax and how to deal with contractions, but no book had prepared me for this. No book had told me how to deal with contractions when there was a threat of being whisked off handcuffed to hospital if I made a noise. The day progressed slowly and painfully. Mary arrived, which made me feel better but didn't eliminate the pain of labor. How do women stand this for days, I wondered, tensely biting the sheets as the contractions increased.

Roll call was at 4 o'clock. Too afraid to make it to the gate, I managed to call the guard as he passed. "I'm not feeling too good. Is it alright if I pass my roll call here?" I tried to look as normal as possible, giving no hint of labor. "Do you need a doctor?" he asked. "No, I'm just tired. A good night's sleep will help." The Mexicans so revere the mother figure that he was sympathetic and passed me.

BORN INTO CAPTIVITY

At 6.30 Mary checked me. I was still only five centimeters dilated: I could tell she was worried. At 7 p.m. she returned from the women's section with Dr Hernandez and Sister Antonia. She told them the situation, and they were all concerned. They had to leave the prison by 8 p.m. and did not want to abandon me in labor. Mary came and checked me again. She looked up at Dr Hernandez and shouted, smiling: "She's fully dilated. The baby's coming."

Suddenly there was much scurrying around, the sterile sheets, betadine, a topical antiseptic, all appeared. Sister Antonia grabbed the flashlight. Mary and Dr Hernandez positioned themselves to help the baby into the world and Charles attempted to make me feel more comfortable. "You can push now."

I started to push, it was hard, it was painful, but it was exhilarating. His head was apparently facing the wrong way, and he was stuck.

"Try squatting, " advised Mary. I got up with Charles's help and pushed. All of a sudden I felt a burning sensation followed by a scream and in a daze I saw a little hanging bundle of slimy flesh and all around me smiling faces.

"It's a boy," Mary cried. And so Sean Albie made it into the world at 7.32, just half an hour before visitors had to leave.

Mary cleaned him off. Dr Hernandez helped me deliver the afterbirth and then they had to leave. They left Charles with his new son, me, the afterbirth and a bed covered in bloody sheets. The mess could wait; now was a time to marvel and be thankful for the miracle. Sister Antonia reappeared with Claudia and Goyo, the prison photographer, and we shot a whole roll of film of Albie at one hour old. Charles cleaned up, waiting till later that night to go and dump the placenta.

SAILING INTO THE ABYSS

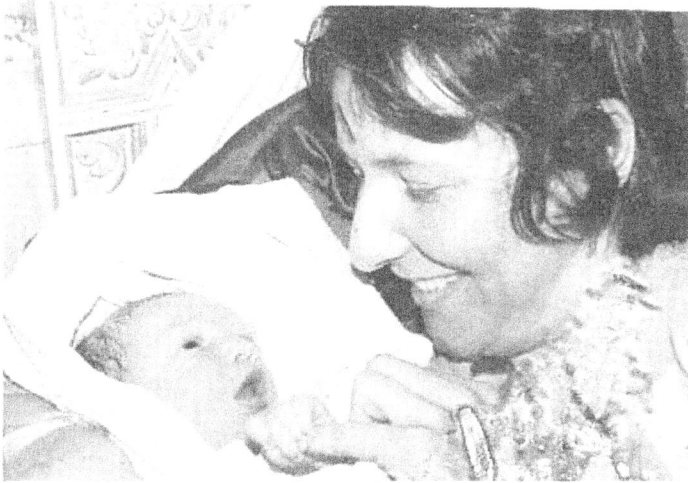

"Hello, world," says Albie.

Albie lay on the bed wide awake for five hours just looking all around, particularly enjoying the lights from the television. I lay there too, happy as can be. Charles and I with the baby between us then attempted to get some sleep.

The following day we had to deal with an irate Director. He came up to our *caraca* furious. Luckily I was fine and obviously healthy, as was our adorable little boy. The Mexicans love children so eventually things quietened down and we were left with our new baby.

The next three months went by with me doing little but playing with Albie. I was thankful for the time, and lack of distractions. No shopping, nowhere to go. I just sat there hanging things up for him to watch, talking to him and gazing at him in never-ending wonder. But having so much uninterrupted time with my baby, I started to feel more vulnerable being imprisoned.

These people had the power to take my baby away. I feared something happening to him and not being able to take him to the hospital or doctor. There had been many babies who had become sick in prison and been sent out. Their mothers were forced to hand them over and then no baby came back, just the news of their death. I cried just at the thought of this. I wouldn't take him into the yard as I was frightened of the various illnesses prevalent, especially meningitis.

He wanted to nurse continuously, which was fine as far as I was concerned, though I did little else. I couldn't imagine how anyone managed to have two children. Cynthia came over to help clean as I seemed to do nothing but nurse and gentle activities such as writing and reading, which I could do while nursing. Eventually I became adept at cleaning and cooking while he continued to nurse.

I wrote in my diary on 18 June: "Guards marched in to take out our back window and block it up." We had no warning. I got upset at the reminder of our lack of rights, which made me realize how vulnerable we were, Charles got so angry I thought they'd throw him in the *tombas*. We had lost our view out over the prison walls to the free world

Mary still visited as there were always pregnant women and the need for pre-natal and post-natal care was strongly evident. She supported my continued nursing as Albie was obviously flourishing. Many of my other friends felt I should be getting him on to a schedule and giving him a supplement. My feelings were that I should give him whatever he wanted and to keep nursing him without supplements as our future was so uncertain. On 27 June he had a slight fever and I was a disaster! When he got better I finally put him into his own bed to sleep, and he slept all night long for the first time. He continued to sleep all night till we left La Mesa. Meanwhile Claudia gave birth to a little girl in Dr Hernandez's private hospital.

SAILING INTO THE ABYSS

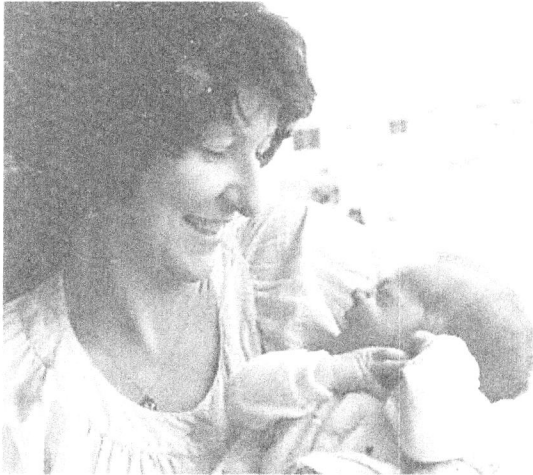

On our balcony with Albie

On 29 July we were notified that our sentence had been revoked, and we were being handed over to the United States authorities. Panic: they separate mothers and babies in the United States. Albie had no papers. I rushed to phone the British Embassy to see what they could do and was told that a representative was coming to see us in the next day or two. We decided to start packing and sent most of our possessions off with Sister Antonia, leaving us just the bare minimum. I began to get more and more neurotic, as images of United States officials trying to take my baby away from me coursed through my brain.

Finally, a Bruce Macintyre from the British Embassy turned up with Dr Hernandez. They went off to find our lawyers and attempt to find out what was happening. Bruce Macintyre succeeded in seeing the Judge and getting our passports back. He saw the United States Embassy and got assurances that we would not be separated. He also wrote a covering letter for Albie until he got his own passport – this was yet another crisis, postponed.

We wanted to baptize Albie before leaving La Mesa. On Friday

13 August we finally did. I dressed him in Claudia's baptism dress of silk and lace that her grandparents, her parents, her siblings and their offspring had used. I felt extremely honored to be able to use it.

Me, Charles and Albie

Arturo was his Godfather and Sister Antonia his Godmother. Arturo appeared yet again with appetizing food and an enormous cake. The ceremony in the little church was exceptionally special, and I was touched by the fact that the church was full.

After the baptism, we had a party in our *caraca* and the cake was taken around the whole prison.

Albie with Claudia in her baptism dress

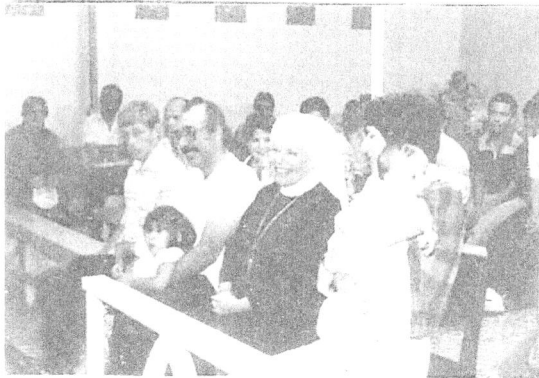

By 31 August we had forgotten about our imminent departure and were again settling into daily life in prison. But at five in the afternoon we heard our voices being called over the loudspeaker. Charles went to investigate, and five minutes after his going, guards arrived to fetch me. I was taken off with nothing but what I was wearing, and Albie wearing nothing but a diaper. Everyone was rushing around to wish us luck. Claudia and Goyo were trying to collect our belongings, but we weren't allowed to take anything with

us, only my purse, which luckily they had not noticed on my arm. Sister Antonia arrived just in time to see us being taken out of the prison into a waiting car. Where were we going? We had no papers, no passports, no money, and no clothes: nothing. I started to panic about Albie's lack of clothes, and Charles became so angry I was afraid he'd get another charge against him. The two young men with us attempted to calm him down as they drove us off, away from Tijuana prison. Where were we being taken to now?

CHAPTER SIXTEEN

FREEDOM

The car drove quickly through the streets of Tijuana. "Where are we going?" I asked our new companions. "It's OK," one of them replied in answer. They couldn't have been more than twenty-five years old. The taller one, who was not driving, said we were being taken to Mexico City, and we were hurrying as we had a flight to catch. Asking him if the British Embassy knew we were coming, he assured us that they did and would be there to meet us, and our money and possessions would be following us. This was the one time I saw the logic of their reasoning, though this was in retrospect. I relaxed and enjoyed the journey. Of course the British Embassy had not been informed, and there was no one there to meet us, but my panicking for five hours would not have made it any better.

Albie stared around in amazement. Not quite three months old, he'd spent all his life in one room with just the occasional trip across the yard, and now he was in a car and an airplane. The stewardess on the plane lent me a blanket to wrap around him. He nursed the entire flight. Luckily, Mary had bought a baby carrier for me to wear a month earlier, so he lay snuggled in it and fell asleep before we arrived in Mexico City. He slept so well at night these days, I hoped he would stay asleep through whatever was to follow. We arrived at Mexico City and stood there waiting for over an hour for a car.

151

FREEDOM

"Where's the British Consul?" I asked, still after sixteen months naively believing the Mexicans.

"Oh, they decided to wait at the Immigration centre. That's where we're going as soon as the car arrives. Don't worry," the tall man replied.

Eventually the car arrived, and off we drove for almost two hours before stopping at a low white building. We had interrupted the journey only for our companion to buy diapers. We walked through a glass door to a desk where a large, pleasant man was filling out papers. He smiled at us, while the young man with us handed him our papers and filled him in with information about us. I was amazed at how cold it was. I assumed as we were further south it would be warmer, not realizing how high we were and that Mexico City sometimes gets snow in the winter.

Once the paperwork was finished, the man behind the desk beckoned for someone to come and fetch Charles. "Can't we stay together?" I asked. The man smiled. "Well, maybe tomorrow we can organize something," he said, "but for now, I'm afraid not." So Charles disappeared, and the man came around from behind the desk and bade me follow him. Albie had woken up by this time and was staring around in amazement. We followed the man to a door which he unlocked; we went through it onto a grass square and then into another one-storeyed building. We walked along a corridor past locked doors with barred windows till we came to the very end. There he unlocked the door, and we followed him in. In front of us was a sink and then a large room with two high and narrow beds. From the high ceiling a naked light bulb shone down over us. Each bed had a mattress but was otherwise uncovered. The man handed me a single coarse brown blanket, smiled apologetically and left, locking the door behind him. I stood there for a time, slightly disorientated, with Albie peering around, now wide awake. Well at least we've got water, I finally concluded, and went to the sink with relief. I needed a drink.

I turned on the tap. There was nothing. No sink at all is better than a sink without any water, I thought bitterly. All I could do now was try to get comfy. Spreading out the hairy brown blanket, I took off my skirt, removed Albie from his carrier and crawled under it. He nursed all night and, in fact, was never again able to sleep through a complete night until his brother was born almost three years later. It was so cold. I just hugged my poor little son all night, wondering what the next day would bring.

After a restless night with the light continually on and Albie nuzzling without stop, I heard the door being unlocked. A woman came in, short and stocky, probably in her mid-fifties. She bade me "Good morning" briskly, not realizing I had a little boy buried under the blanket. I thought it was time she found out. Pulling aside the blanket, I revealed his little body curled up next to mine, almost as naked as the day he was born.

"Oh, the poor little boy! Where are his clothes?" She turned on me with an accusatory glare, and Albie looked up at her, his deep blue eyes never failing to produce a smile.

Her voice changed. "Hang on, I'll be right back." She rushed off and returned about three-quarters of an hour later with a few baby clothes. I dressed Albie and together he and I followed the woman down the corridor and out into the grassy courtyard.

At 8 o'clock we were called for breakfast. The dining room was a large room with three long tables that would seat approximately forty people each. I was alone with Albie. I took my aluminum plate with a boiled egg and a spoonful of cold lentils and sat down, Albie nursing again. So this was my new home: the kitchen stretched beyond the dining room and I heard voices the other side of the wall. I assumed the men must be behind it. Hearing my name, I went to the wall. "Bridget, Bridget, are you there?" It was Charles. I smiled.

"Yes. What's happening? How are you?"

"Fine ... How about you? Listen: send a request to see the Director and we'll try to get to see the Consul."

"Oh, I hope we're not here long. I'm all alone here."

"I've got to go and eat now. Send your request in, OK?"

"OK." Begrudgingly I let him go, hearing many voices. What was I meant to do now? Albie was restless, so we walked around the square. I told Albie he'd see his Daddy soon, that we'd all be somewhere pleasant soon; round and round the square till he fell asleep. I went back to my cell and sat there; nothing to read, nothing to look at and no one to talk to except Albie. I lay down holding him in my arms till I heard the guard come back in.

"I want to see the Director," I told her.

"Oh, it's too late to put a request in now," she answered. "You can ask tomorrow."

What a long day. Would it never end? I walked and walked and talked to Albie all day long. The following morning I was ready to put in my request to see the Director. At 11 o'clock a guard appeared and called me. I followed him back out to the entrance hall we'd been at two nights earlier. Was it only two days? It was an interminable two days. Charles appeared with six or seven other men of different nationalities: a couple of black men and an interesting trio, who turned out to be Italians, very flamboyantly dressed with punk hairdos and stylized movements. I was so pleased to see Charles that I fell upon him. "I'm going to go crazy here. How long are we going to be here?"

"I don't know. I've met a couple of great guys; there's a Belgian guy who has been here for months. He says we just have to keep making our demands."

We decided to tell the Director we wanted our money and possessions from Tijuana, and we wanted to contact our Embassy; I also needed things for the baby immediately.

SAILING INTO THE ABYSS

Finally, we were called in. "Yes?" The Director sat without looking up. I stood up and went toward him. I wanted to make sure he saw Albie. I wanted him to realize he had a baby in his cells. It worked. We made our requests. He informed us that we would have to wait till the next day to call the Embassy, but he said that if I made out a list of what I needed for the baby he would send someone to get it. He also claimed that he would investigate what had happened to our possessions and money.

Thus began our daily routine: breakfast at 8 o'clock, consisting of a hard-boiled egg and sometimes some cold lentils and sometimes not, then the waiting around until it was the time to go and see the Director. We were allowed only one phone call a day so we'd either phone the Embassy or try someone in Tijuana. We called our lawyers, we called Noreen in San Diego one day while Sister Antonia was visiting, and that was a good day. When we ran out of reasons to see the Director, we got permission to visit with each other for half an hour a day. Charles was able to play with Albie, the only half-hour of the day when he wasn't in my arms.

Lunch at 1 o'clock consisted of more cold lentils with either a small piece of meat or potatoes. We had nothing to do, no books, no games and so the afternoon passed unbearably slowly till 5 o'clock when we had the evening meal of more cold lentils. We usually went to sleep at 7 o'clock.

Albie was constantly in my arms. The bed was too high and too narrow to leave him lying alone, and there was nowhere else for him to go. At night I had to keep him covered and nestling in my arms. I was worried about him falling out of bed, but even more worrying were the mosquitoes. The Immigration building was very close to a large body of stagnant water and there were more mosquitoes there than I'd ever seen before. I cradled little Albie, trying to shield him and mostly succeeding, but I got my arms so badly bitten that I had to see a doctor. Despite my best efforts, one night one of his little hands fell out of the cover and became thoroughly covered in a mass of bites.

I was only alone for a couple of days; after that various groups of mainly Salvadoran women came and went. They were so desperate, these poor women. Most of them had somehow made it to the United States border only to be arrested and handed over to the Mexicans who had thrown them in jail. Their jailers would take their few possessions, crowd them into coaches and then bus them to the Mexico City Detention Centre where they'd have to stay for anything from a few hours to a couple of days. From there they would be crowded into more coaches and driven to the Guatemalan border. What happened to them at the border I hated to think. They were so despondent, and yet when they saw my baby all they wanted was to touch him. He could make their eyes alive again as they thought of their own children and their own early days as mothers. I felt anguish. I was so sorry for these women, but I was even more afraid of my baby becoming sick in this place, where I knew absolutely no one who could help us. So I shied away from my fellow prisoners with their woeful eyes, their rasping coughs and their depressing tales. Fortunately the guard then left me alone in my room, using the larger cells with twenty beds to house the Salvadorans.

Occasionally there were a few women from other places, but never for long. There was a girl from the Dominican Republic who had just been on holiday and wasn't even sure why she'd be been picked up. Then a black girl who wouldn't say where she was from; they'd tried to deport her to the United States and to Belize, but she wasn't accepted at either. She was very sullen, spoke no Spanish and had little interest in speaking English with me either. The only person there for longer than four days was a crazy Colombian girl who wandered around the square naked, talking to herself and issuing orders to the guards.

SAILING INTO THE ABYSS

On our fourth day at the Detention Centre we had to make a trip to the downtown Immigration Office. Straight after eating my cold hard-boiled egg, I was taken to the entrance hall, put into a van with six men including Charles, and driven off. It was a long and uncomfortable trip and Albie hated it and screamed. As he screamed I would become tense, and he would pick up on my vibrations and scream more. My poor little son, who had never cried before leaving Tijuana, now showed how healthy his lungs were.

Driving downtown we saw big buildings, bars and restaurants. It was so long since I'd seen big city shops. The main Immigration Office was off a busy street in the heart of Mexico City. When we arrived, the police took everyone out of the van and herded us toward cells that looked like dungeons. One of the guards looked at me and my baby and kindly decided not to put us in them. Instead, we were taken with Charles upstairs to wait in the office where our papers were being processed. As we sat there, we could see that the whole pageant was a study in wasted energy, a giant bureaucracy at work. We sat and watched offices full of men and women filling out endless forms and filing them in a wall full of endless filing cabinets. A lot of other people sat around a table waiting to be questioned.

We were there seven hours; six hours just sitting waiting. Mr Whitton from the Embassy arrived with clothes for Charles and me, towels and baby clothes and diapers. It was so comforting to see him again. He was very British, treating us with total respect, as he had from the first meeting in Tijuana. He apologized for not being able to get to visit us, but there were only four of them in the office and they were exceptionally busy. He had, unfortunately, forgotten to bring us any books, which was what I needed more than anything. He had been in touch with our lawyers and they were sending our passports to him. Albie would need to get a Mexican passport as he could not get a British one quickly, since Charles and

FREEDOM

I were not married. He was applying to the judge in Tijuana for our money, but wasn't optimistic about our chances of getting it returned.

Evening came, and we returned to the dreaded Detention Centre. I hated the place, but the guards were all kind to me. They fetched me milk to drink and fruit to eat, as I was worried about my own milk supply. I was so glad Albie was not yet on supplements, as there was nowhere I could have sterilized bottles or heated water. They'd stopped locking me in at nights as one night I'd had a nightmare about something happening to Albie and no one could hear me screaming for help.

This had happened to one of the Salvadoran women: an older woman, who had spent the day sitting on her bed looking white as a ghost, that night had a spasm and stopped breathing. Her companions screamed for two awful hours until help eventually arrived. I made a big fuss about my equally precarious situation, and they no longer locked me in at night after that.

Every day I was becoming more and more depressed and would burst into tears at every little thing. I think Charles sometimes dreaded his half-hour with us as he felt so helpless. I remembered Sister Antonia telling me about saying to a woman with a baby in prison on one of her first visits, "It must be so hard to be in here with your baby." The woman responded, "It would be so much harder without my baby."

I understood that. Albie was all that kept me sane but at the same time was the reason I worried so much. I talked to him for hours, telling him stories and singing him songs. One day they came to spray the cells against mosquitoes, but they'd forgotten to tell me. The first I knew was that I heard a terrible noise and then a smell. My eyes began to hurt, and Albie started to cough. I looked into the corridor and saw a huge tank-like machine advancing toward me. There were men in protective suits and helmets spraying something.

SAILING INTO THE ABYSS

I ran out wrapping a towel around Albie's head and sat sobbing on the grass listening to his labored breathing, petrified that he'd been poisoned. Another day while I was downtown at the Immigration Office a Cuban girl stole everything that the Consul had bought for Albie. I was devastated as she had seemed to be someone I could relate to, she spoke English and was not poor like most of the prisoners. When I reported the theft everyone was searched, which made me feel guilty. The Cuban girl was actually being released and on her way out when one of the guards took her case. Inside were all Albie's clothes.

Charles was enjoying a far better time, as the men were more mixed. There were Europeans and Americans as well as the refugees from Central America. They played cards and soccer, and spent hours talking and discussing various topics.

We had another two trips downtown: one to get Albie a passport; the second was to visit the British Embassy and fill out some forms. After finishing our business at the Embassy and before the immigration van returned to pick us up, we asked our guard if we could walk back to the main office. He agreed, not realizing what a treat it was for us to walk down streets with normal everyday people, looking into shop windows and soaking up the smells and sounds of a big city.

On 21 September we had our fourth trip downtown. We were informed we were leaving the next day and asked where we wanted to go. We opted for Belize, a former British colony, as we needed no visas; it was English speaking and the journey wouldn't be too long or too expensive. It was a place I'd always wanted to visit. We were told that, although we were being deported, as parents of a Mexican child we could return to Mexico at any time.

Knowing we were leaving the next day, I began to relax and sat there watching these people in whose country we had been living for seventeen months now: kind and corrupt, a mixture of contradictions. I translated for a Frenchman who had come from the Detention Centre with us. He had been stopped outside his hotel and asked for his papers; because he didn't have them on him, he was taken off to jail. When getting out of jail, he was told he would be deported. The reason? Because he'd been in jail! A Chinese businessman had made a day trip to Tijuana during his Californian holiday. He'd been robbed of all his money and papers so had been imprisoned for having no papers and taken to Mexico City. He spoke no Spanish or English except "Yes please." He tried again and again to tell his story by actions. What would happen to him? We would never know as we were leaving.

I got up eagerly on the morning of 22 September and endured the trip downtown, crowded into the van with Albie screaming. We were allowed to spend the day in the British Embassy, drinking tea and reading magazines. Our friend Mr Whitton bought diapers for the trip and bade us an affectionate farewell. At 6 p.m. we boarded the bus for Chetumal, along with three men from Belize and two immigration officers. It was a 22-hour trip, and although I was delighted about our imminent release I was also dreading the journey. Fortunately Albie slept quite a lot and the men from Belize sitting behind us helped entertain him when he was awake. The Immigration officers drank beer and laughed together as if they were off on holiday. The bus trundled on through the night. I had a hard time sleeping with Albie feeding on me all night, but eventually the sun came up. Charles took his son while I slept. When I awoke the sun was creeping higher and higher into the sky. Out of the windows lush green fields flashed by; we passed small huts and black-haired barefoot children. Life looked bright and good.

Late that afternoon we drove into Chetumal, a large town on the Mexican–Belize border. We stopped at the bus station, and another immigration car came to meet us. Along with the immigration officers and men from Belize, we piled in and drove off, straight to the border. The Mexicans looked at our passports, smiled at Albie's Mexican passport, then waved us on. We looked across the bridge spanning the Rio Hondo that separates Mexico from Belize. Nervously we looked back, but the Mexicans had already forgotten us. We walked across the bridge. It was 5.33 on the afternoon of 23 September 1981. As we approached the border post we heard the murmur of the river under the bridge; the strains of reggae music wafting from the little community of Santa Elena, interspersed with a word or two of lilting English. We reached the border and nervously handed over our passports. The immigration officer stamped them and returned them.

We were free in Belize. Charles and I turned to look at each other almost in a trance. Albie gurgled; we turned to look at our small son, who was born in captivity and was now for the first time in his young life free.

CHAPTER SEVENTEEN

EPILOGUE

I wrote this manuscript when Albie was three years old and my youngest son just a few months. Then life became busy, and I set it aside. A couple of years later I went to Spain to help out my sister Judy, who had her own legal problems, and I took the manuscript hoping to have time to work on it. With five children to look after, the "spare time" never materialized and I ended up leaving the manuscript there. Recently my sister found it, read it and suggested publishing it. For me, rereading it was very emotional but I agreed that it was a story that should be published. She also suggested adding a chapter to update what had happened to Sister Antonia in the last thirty years, and how I, looking back as my son celebrated his 30th birthday, felt about my experiences now.

I was lucky enough to remain close to Sister Antonia for the three years after leaving Tijuana, as the Mexican authorities had told us that as parents of a Mexican child we were welcome back in Mexico. I was able to observe her from the "other side" as she rushed around getting all she possibly could for her "sons" and "daughters." I never minded that she was always rushing when I saw her, as I knew just how crucial it was to those in La Mesa to have her there, and I was in the outside world where time rushed by as one lived one's life.

Shortly after we left, Ronald Reagan, the then President of the

162

US, wrote to Sister Antonia praising her "devotion to a calling beyond the ordinary." I never thought I would find myself sharing sentiments with a man such as Reagan, but with this I fully agreed. I was glad he had recognized her total unselfishness in helping those in so much need.

In April 1986 I sailed away with my family, heading back toward England. Sister Antonia performed a boat blessing on our yacht before we left, which was a particularly memorable and touching occasion. And it was with mixed feelings we said goodbye to Tijuana and all the friends we had made during our time there. I had written this manuscript before leaving, but what I wanted to do more than anything was to return when my children were grown and write the life story of Sister Antonia.

Over the next decade, it was hard to get any news from Tijuana; we were working our way back to England, so spent some years teaching school in Central America and home-schooling our children. These were the years before the internet, so communication was dependent on a not particularly reliable mail service. I missed the news of Sister Antonia meeting Pope John Paul II on Mothers' Day in 1990; and of her meeting with Mother Teresa, who visited her in Tijuana in 1991. I was sent news of her stopping the riot in Tijuana jail in 1994, when hungry prisoners in the punishment cells managed to get keys and a gun off a guard. Quickly, large numbers of heavily armed riot police were assembled ready to storm the prison, but before they did Sister Antonia arrived. She had been outside the prison, but when she heard about the riot she rushed back and demanded to be let in. The guards were reluctant to allow her in, fearing she would be shot, but she talked to the Director, Señor Duarte, on the phone, and knowing her well he knew she might be able to prevent a massacre. She entered the pitch-black prison (the electricity had been turned off) on her own and unarmed, and talked to her "sons" and got them to hand over their weapons, then went with their spokesman to tell Duarte of their complaints.

It was hard to imagine a riot, but over the years since we had left, La Mesa prison had grown, and with its growth came an increase in crime, so the prison had become more crowded and with that the problems had grown. Señor Duarte had become the Director in 1992; he was a law professor and was known as a fair man who believed in dialogue and restraint. Sadly he was dragged from his car and assassinated in 1995.

Over the years, Sister Antonia accumulated more helpers as more and more people wanted to be involved with her. I received news of her mission and always inspiring stories of achievements made by the prisoners; they would always make me smile as I could see her rushing in to tell me about them, her face beaming with joy. The Bishop of San Diego had urged her to invite others to join her, and the Bishop of Tijuana also had told her that she should form a religious community. She believed that many women, as they grew older and their own children had moved on with their lives, had a lot to give, so she called her community the Eudist Servants of the 11th Hour, the 11th Hour symbolizing the many women who in their later years want to give something back, as she had. All the sisters are financially independent with their own healthcare and make their vows for a year, renewable annually. They operate a mission close to La Mesa, which is a refuge for women leaving the prison, as well as women visiting inmates. The sisters live in a convent close by, though some remain living in San Diego, traveling to Tijuana each day.

In the year 2000, Charles and I had finally sailed back to England and were working while our sons finished their education. With a home, internet connection and phone I could reconnect with my old friends in southern California. It was with horror that I received the news in August 2002 that 2,000 prisoners were handcuffed and moved out of La Mesa to a new prison 50 miles east of Tijuana. During one day, hundreds of women and children who had lived there as families were sent out of the prison, carrying their belongings. Later that day the bulldozers entered and destroyed the village within La Mesa, preparing the way to build a conventional US-type prison.

In 2005 I heard that a book was being written about the life of Sister Antonia, now known as Mother Antonia. I was disappointed, as it had remained my dream that I would be the one to write the story; but when I read the book *The Prison Angel* by Mary Jordan and Kevin Sullivan, I realized that it was a story that needed to be told now, and they did a tremendous job and it is a terrific book.

Living and working back in England, with our sons living their own lives, I was able to take holidays, so have returned to San Diego on a few occasions. The first trip was just before the book was published and I was lucky enough to have a delightful evening with Sister Antonia and the Olesens. It was almost twenty years since I had seen her and I had certainly aged, but she looked identical to the last time I'd seen her: the same smile that warmed all who were in her presence and the same energy. She talked excitedly about how she was now able to visit the town jails as well as La Mesa, and how with all the help she was receiving she could help so many more people. She told me what an honor it had been to meet the Pope and Mother Teresa, but the real joy to her was that in honoring her they were honoring her "sons" and "daughters" in La Mesa and in the other jails.

In 2005 Sister Antonia was inducted into the Hall of Fame for Caring Americans; she said, "Happiness does not depend on where you live; I don't have a lot of pleasures, but I have a lot of joy."

In September 2008 I was upset to see scenes of rioting in the prison. I was able to watch it live on the internet and my heart felt for all those involved. The official figure was 23 dead and 70 wounded. Sister Antonia was the only outsider allowed in; she was quoted as blaming overcrowding and the death of an inmate, allegedly at the hands of a guard, for causing the riots. "I think we have to look at this situation and find out how we can have men in prison in a more humane way. That's one of the big steps," she said. At the time of the riots there were 9,000 inmates whereas the prison was built for a maximum of 3,000.

In 2010 I visited San Diego again, and while I was there a big celebration was underway in Tijuana as the city officials renamed the avenue in front of La Mesa "Avenida Madre Antonia Brenner." At the same time Jody Hammond, a documentary film-maker, was making *La Mama*, a movie about Sister Antonia's work. It is a wonderful movie, narrated by the actress Susan Sarandon, and I did an interview on it and was proud to have been a part of it. During this visit Sister Antonia's extraordinary energy amazed me yet again. She was trying to fit in a visit to San Diego so we could get together, and she told me that she would call in the morning: at 5 a.m. I was woken by my phone. I then remembered she was always up at that time, even though she rarely got to bed before 11 or 12 p.m. She managed in a very full day to get up to see me for a wonderful hour before rushing off to do a million things.

On my last visit to southern California she had finally moved out of the prison due to her deteriorating health; she was immensely sad about it, and although her family in the US wanted her to move closer to them, she became anxious if she was too far away from Tijuana, so she moved into the Convent where she had help but could still visit La Mesa.

Her life could end at any time, but while she can still drag herself around she will continue to help those she can; and her smile, as marvelous as ever, continues to brighten people's lives.

CHAPTER EIGHTEEN

LOOKING BACK

So here I am, thirty years on, looking back at the events of that time, older and wiser but still struggling financially. I do know that from the moment my son was born, I decided I would never do anything illegal again, never risk that my son could be taken away from me. By the time I was freed I had a family and had spent over a year with Sister Antonia, so though financially poorer I felt infinitely richer.

I believe the drug laws around the world only help the criminal gangs, as did alcohol prohibition in the US in the 1920s. The Mexican drug cartels are not afraid of the police or the army; the only thing that they are scared of is legalization. Legalization would give control to the government and money generated by sales and taxes could be used for education and clinics for those abusing drugs. It would keep young people away from criminals and mean that many young people would not end up with criminal records.

I know I was very lucky to have been in La Mesa when I was; a few years earlier, before Sister Antonia moved there, it was a remarkably different and much scarier place. After we left, overcrowding became more of a problem, bringing tensions and an increase in violence and corruption with it. In our eighteen months I witnessed virtually no violence, less than one would find in any small village.

I learned a lot in my time there: I realized that prisons everywhere are mainly full of poor people from disadvantaged backgrounds, and the chances are that their families will also suffer as a result of imprisonment of the father or mother, son or daughter. Rehabilitation cannot possibly happen when everything that makes us human—the love of our friends and family, a supportive society—is taken from us. La Mesa showed there was another way. Corruption, drugs and guns within the prison after we left are not an argument that it didn't work. The argument is that it should have been monitored better, and corruption not allowed to take such a hold. It is better for men and women to be able to keep contact with their children, to help them with their studies, to show them that, despite being in prison for their crimes, they are able to strive to lead a useful life. Imprisonment is a punishment in itself, and anyone who doesn't understand that has never been imprisoned.

I was very lucky to have had the support of my family who organized my lawyers and managed to secure the *caraca* we lived in. I had old friends who sent books, visited and wrote letters. I met wonderful people who have remained close friends to this day: Noreen, the Olesens and my fantastic midwife Mary, who also delivered my second son. But certainly I feel incredibly privileged for the time spent with Sister Antonia. There is not a day when I don't think of her, and in my own little way I try to be more like her; try to stop myself judging others; to smile and be positive about every situation, and be kind and loving to others. An awful lot of the time I fail dismally, but her smile stays in my head and I keep trying.

If you enjoyed this book, please leave a review on Amazon

SAILING INTO THE ABYSS (TRUE SMUGGLING ADVENTURE)

If you would like to know more about Bridget's sister Judy buy her book Mr.Nice & Mrs Marks available on Amazon.

Printed in Dunstable, United Kingdom